Detail of
"Mancos Black-on-White" bowl.
Anasazi Heritage Center.

THE ANASAZI

Why did they leave? Where did they go?

A panel discussion at the
Anasazi Heritage Center, Dolores, Colorado,
sponsored by the Bureau of Land Management as part of
the "Four Corners Tribute," June 19, 1990

MODERATOR
Dr. W. James Judge

PANEL MEMBERS
Dr. David A. Breternitz
Dr. Linda S. Cordell
Dr. George J. Gumerman
Leigh Jenkins
Edmund J. Ladd
Dr. William Lipe

EDITOR
Jerold G. Widdison

Southwest Natural and Cultural Heritage Association
Albuquerque, New Mexico

Acknowledgments

The efforts of many individuals and groups have made this publication possible. The professional staff of the Anasazi Heritage Center arranged the panel discussion, with valuable assistance provided by staff members of the state and area offices of the Bureau of Land Management in Colorado, New Mexico, Utah, and Arizona. Editorial services and partial funds for publication were contributed by Southwest Natural and Cultural Heritage Association. Additional publication funds were generously made available by the Bureau of Land Management and Western Gas Supply Company of Denver, Colorado.

ISBN 1-879343-07-X

Maps by Jerold G. Widdison
Typography by Prototype

Contents

Foreword

Shela A. McFarlin
Director
Anasazi Heritage Center

What Happened to the Anasazi?
Why Did They Leave?
Where Did They Go?

These are not just academic questions for archaeologists studying the prehistoric people of the Four Corners region. Many others of us—students, teachers, tourists, residents—stand in awe at the great cliff dwellings of the Anasazi Indians and want to know more of their story. "Who were these people?" "Why, when, and how did they live here?" "Why did they go away?"

And further, "Were the Anasazi the ancestors of the present-day Pueblo Indians?" All such questions come readily to mind at many places in the Four Corners. Here the land is dotted with thousands of sites where the Anasazi lived, yet none of today's Pueblo Indians inhabit the area.

People have flocked to see Anasazi ruins for more than a century, ever since the spectacular ancient "cities" and the finely made baskets and pottery of the Anasazi became known. During that time, too, archaeologists have recorded thousands of sites and have excavated a few hundred of them. Through time, new technologies (such as archaeomagnetism) and new approaches to understanding cultural change have given rise to innumerable technical reports, including several "explanations" of why the Anasazi abandoned the Four Corners area about A.D. 1300. Yet even after years of study, the abandonment/migration of the Anasazi remains an overarching question of Southwest archaeology.

To review the various hypotheses, and perhaps to spark new ideas, a unique round table or panel discussion was held at the Anasazi Heritage Center on June 19, 1990. The discussion, which was open to the public and which appears here in published form, presented the views of five distinguished archaeologists and two especially knowledgeable representatives of the modern-day Pueblo Indians. The purpose of the discussion was, of course, to increase the public's knowledge of the Anasazi past.

The round table was one expression of a new nationwide effort to highlight the American heritage—the Bureau of Land Management's initiative called "Adventures in the Past." The intent of the "Adventures" program is to protect the vast archaeological and historic resources of the nation's public lands from looting and vandalism. But as the term "adventures" implies, the same resources are to be tapped for public enjoyment, enrichment, and firsthand ventures into the unknown.

The "Four Corners Tribute," held June 19–21, 1990, at the Anasazi Heritage Center near Dolores, Colorado, was the kickoff event for "Adventures." The "Four Corners Tribute" was in part a celebration featuring exhibits, "living history" demonstrations, and media events, but it also included the "Four Corners Governors Conference on Partners for the Past." More than a hundred community and tribal leaders, land managers, and scientific and humanities professionals met for three days to devise a strategy for the 21st century—a strategy for the coordinated management, protection, and interpretation of the rich cultural heritage of the Four Corners.

As part of the "Tribute," the panel discussion brought the puzzle of the Anasazi disappearance to public attention. Several hundred people, in fact, gave their *full* attention for two hours as the seven panelists offered their explanations and answered audience questions on the fate of the Anasazi.

Who Were the Anasazi?

Archaeologists apply the Navajo word *anasazi* (interpreted variously as "ancient ones," "ancient enemies," etc.) to the prehistoric Indians who lived in the Four Corners area between approximately A.D. 1 and A.D. 1300. For more than a millennium these remarkably successful people, relying primarily on corn agriculture, lived in large and small villages spread widely over the mesa-and-canyon landscape. Their irrigated fields and garden plots were important achievements, yet it is their architecture that remains most impressive. Multistoried pueblos and cliff dwellings are sometimes magnificent and sometimes quite puzzling in both style and adaptive features. Some of the Anasazi structures dominate the landscape, while other buildings and constructions are more subtle—such as granaries in rock niches and stairways etched into canyon walls. Other "signatures" of the Anasazi include fine trade goods, bone and wooden tools, and beautiful ceramics—all creative in design, varied in style, and well crafted.

Various kinds of evidence—ranging from rock art to ceremonial rooms—reveal the importance to the Anasazi of social rituals and their strong recognition of seasons and astronomical events. While the Anasazi consistently lived in small family units throughout all their history, they also sustained ties among larger groups, and they built extensive trade networks. By A.D. 1200, villages had become veritable towns, some containing 400 to 600 or more rooms, some of them organized around plazas and most having towers, perimeter walls, and internal divisions.

Yet the Anasazi success eventually came to an end. By the year A.D. 1300, the Anasazi had in fact disappeared from the immediate Four Corners area. So complete was their exodus that archaeologists wondered for a time whether the people had gone away in large migrations. Now, however, the abandonment of the Anasazi has come to be understood quite differently.

Why Did the Anasazi Leave?

Questions of cause and effect were at the heart of the round table discussion, just as they have been since the first archaeological probings of the Four Corners area a century ago. Were the Anasazi driven out of the region? Did they leave for areas where life was easier or where it was thought to be easier? Did environmental changes or societal difficulties cause them to leave?

No one knows precisely what happened, and it may be that several interrelated causes were effective. But whatever the case, for many years the explanations offered for the Anasazi abandonment have sorted themselves into two categories, the "push" theories and the "pull" theories.

Some of the oldest but still-current push explanations, as Dave Breternitz

points out in the discussion, have to do with proven or inferred environmental changes, especially variations in climate. Tree-ring studies have indicated the occurrence of a prolonged drought in the Four Corners area between A.D. 1276 and 1299. Deforestation, colder temperatures, arroyo entrenchment, lowered water tables, and shortages of arable land may have been related to the drought. All have been proposed as local causes, at least, for Anasazi dislocations or relocations.

Equally old to Southwest archaeology are explanations having to do with warfare. Warfare—which might have arisen from the competition of newcomers such as Athapaskan or Shoshonean interlopers—has been suggested by certain features of Anasazi architecture, such as walled cities, sites that are obviously defensive in location, and towers that might have served for defense. Warfare as a cause of Anasazi abandonment has been recognized by some archaeologists and disavowed by others, but it will not go away as an explanation.

Other push hypotheses have to do with what might be called social dynamics. In the desertion of their homeland, the Anasazi may have been responding to pressures of increasingly crowded villages, or to rapidly spreading epidemic diseases, or to archaic social institutions. Whatever the case, it is not likely that everyone moved away at once. Quite likely the causes of abandonment were mixed and varied from community to community and from time to time. George Gumerman especially mentions the organization of individual Anasazi communities. Some communities, he indicates, may have been considerably better able than others to deal with the difficulties of town life in times of prolonged drought or other environmental stresses.

For all the long list of push explanations, the panelists have also recognized the possibility of pull situations. Dave Breternitz comments on the "bright lights" theory, the idea that opportunities and attractions outside the immediate Four Corners area were instrumental in drawing the Anasazi to what had previously been only the southern margins of their world. Such lures may have included a modified social organization in southern Anasazi settlements and, perhaps, a new religious and artistic cult. Bill Lipe is particularly interested in what he calls "stronger communities" and "new religious systems" in southern villages, as suggested by pueblos there that had plaza orientations and relatively few kivas.

The discussion also makes it clear that archaeologists do not merely speculate these theories. Instead, everything that has been proposed has been based on painstaking field studies. Excavations and investigations of many kinds—always focused on specific research problems—have provided answers as well as theories. It is certainly clear that the movements and relocations of the Anasazi were "adaptive responses" and conscious decisions. Our understanding of that fact now seems broader and deeper than it once was.

It is also increasingly apparent that mass migrations of the Anasazi did not occur. Rather, what happened was a dwindling away of families and communities (one might say the people were exercising cultural options) during times of social and environmental stress.

Where Did the Anasazi Go?

The panelists have few doubts where the Anasazi went. Convincing arguments were presented long ago that the Anasazi did not simply die or disappear from their abandoned communities; rather, they moved southward to the Rio Grande valley of New Mexico, to the Ácoma-Zuni area, and to the Hopi mesas of Arizona. No direct or simple process was this, yet the truth of it is revealed by numerous threads of continuity between the Anasazi and today's Pueblo Indian societies. The threads are tangled by historic contacts (the coming of the Spaniards in the 16th and 17th centuries had enormous consequences) and by cultural and linguistic differences among the several pueblos; yet there can be little doubt that the Pueblo Indians are descended from people of the Anasazi tradition. On this point, Linda Cordell emphasizes both the movement and the reconcentration of the Anasazi in New Mexico, movement southward and eastward from the Four Corners heartland.

Detail of "Mancos Black-on-White" bowl. Anasazi Heritage Center.

For panelists Leigh Jenkins and Ed Ladd, representing the present-day Hopi and Zuni pueblos, the answer to the question is obvious—they *are* the Anasazi. The Hopi feel strongly that the Anasazi were ancestral Hopi peoples, and, as

Leigh points out, they still carry on traditions and ceremonies reaching back to the times of clan migrations. Ed Ladd, expressing the Zuni perspective, also illuminates the role of Pueblo oral tradition in explaining the cultural past.

Meanwhile, archaeologists have by no means exhausted possible explanations nor the field work needed to verify them. Keeping in mind the geographic span of Anasazi archaeology and the decades of research already accomplished, these scientists anticipate future examination of a wide range of problem areas. As the panelists mention in closing their discussion, some research will focus on detailing the abandonment processes that occurred within individual sites. Specific questions might be, for example, "Which pots were left and which were removed to new homes, and why?" "Under what conditions did the departing Indians burn or not burn their houses?" But on the broader end of the research spectrum, the archaeologists plan to expand comparative analyses, to identify regional patterns, and to review behavioral and cross-cultural studies.

As it happened, the panel discussion stirred a desire to reexamine Pueblo oral tradition in relationship to archaeology. One research need, several panelists agreed, was to "evaluate rather than dismiss" oral tradition such as clan migration myths.

The exchange of views among the panelists was indicative of something else, too. As George Gumerman pointed out, a few years ago an event such as this would not have occurred. Archaeologists are now doing better at reporting their results to the public and at offering direct participation. Certainly a growing appreciation of Anasazi culture is reflected by, and must emerge from, the panel discussion. Now perhaps we are nearer than ever before to viewing the Anasazi as people living their lives in complex cultural and physical environments.

If so, we may also notice something pertinent to our own lives. The Anasazi faced and resolved problems in essentially the same marginal environment of the Southwest that we inhabit today. Surely it is reasonable that a knowledge of their lives might help us examine our own ways of solving problems. And while we are doing that, might we not also find appreciation for the heritage and lifeways

Detail of "Tusayan White Ware" potsherd. From Black Mesa, Arizona.

of the modern Pueblo Indians?

Finally, the round table may help us be aware of the need to preserve the traces of the past. While the "Adventures/Tribute" was planned as a celebration of the Anasazi past, it was also a recognition of the great efforts required to manage the physical remnants scattered across the land. The need was aptly stated by Leigh Jenkins when he noted that many prehistoric cultural resources of the Southwest are part and parcel of the Pueblo Indian heritage. Resources, he said, certainly originated with a particular Indian tribe or tradition. Yet in a wider sense, as he added, now "they're *everybody's* heritage."

SHELA A. McFARLIN has been director of the Anasazi Heritage Center since 1985. She holds a master's degree in anthropology from Michigan State University, and she has been involved with public archaeology and field work in the western states, Michigan, East Africa, and Israel.

Introduction

Robert Moore
Colorado State Director of the Bureau of Land Management

Good evening. It gives me a lot of pleasure to be here tonight to see what will happen when we get a tableful of archaeologists together. Our panelists are all very knowledgeable on the subject of the Anasazi culture, yet it may be difficult for them to agree on anything at all. One reason is tonight's topic, which is certainly not a new subject. Mainly it's been one of a lot of questions being asked and not many being answered, at least not being answered in a public forum.

The Anasazi ruins of the Four Corners have fascinated and intrigued the public for over a hundred years. And during that same time the study of archaeology has changed very greatly. It has, in fact, been transformed from only the recovery of artifacts for museums and private collectors to a sophisticated, complex practice of both scientific method and creative art.

Although we're finding out more and more about the lifestyle of the Anasazi, and although we have come to appreciate their success for over a thousand years in a harsh environment, many questions remain unanswered. No one can visit Cliff Palace, Sand Canyon, or Grand Gulch without asking, "What happened to the Anasazi? Why did they leave? Where did they go?" And maybe even, "Why didn't they come back?"

Now for an historic evening. We have several prominent Southwest archaeologists with us to resolve these questions, perhaps once and for all. We may get the definitive answer right here tonight.

In a moment I'm going to introduce the moderator for this evening's "debate,"

Detail of "Mesa Verde Black-on-White" bowl. Anasazi Heritage Center.

Dr. Jim Judge. But first, for the audience and for our experts, I'll cover the ground rules. Dr. Judge and his experts will begin with their summaries or testimony, using evidence and perhaps their own questions to answer the topic question, "What happened to the Anasazi?" . . . Is it possible they'll all agree on one line of thought? What do you think?

Later on, after the experts have had an opportunity to present their remarks, we'll open up for audience questions. We have a microphone available in the center aisle for questions about the Anasazi or about archaeology or related topics that our experts can answer. No question will be ignored. Our panel has all the answers that inquiring minds want to know. [*Turning to the panel*] Does that come as news to you all?

I'm going to start by introducing Dr. Judge, and he will introduce the other panelists.

Dr. Jim Judge's interests in the cultural and natural environment stem from his upbringing in the national parks in the Rocky Mountain West. After graduating from Phillips Exeter Academy and after serving four years as a Marine Corps pilot, he earned a bachelor's degree in political science and spent two years teaching in Ecuador. Dr. Judge received his Ph.D. in anthropology from the University of New Mexico in 1970, and he then began a teaching career in archaeology at Colorado State University. He later returned to the faculty of the University of New Mexico, where he directed the Chaco Project for the National Park Service from 1977 to 1985. Dr. Judge currently directs the Fort Burgwin Research Center and educational facility of Southern Methodist University, located near Taos, New Mexico.

And now for Dr. Judge and the "great debate."

ROBERT MOORE is Colorado state director of the Bureau of Land Management (BLM). He previously directed the BLM Service Center, which provides technical and developmental services for the agency nationwide. Mr. Moore received the Department of the Interior's Distinguished Service Award in 1988.

Jim Judge

The subject of this symposium or debate, or whatever it might be called, is "Where did the Anasazi go?" and "What happened to the Anasazi?" Over the past week or so, I've let several people know that we're having this debate, just as a kind of trial balloon to find out what people might think about such questions. And I've found out such things as, "The Anasazi left because of back taxes," and "They were construction workers who built Mesa Verde and then moved on."

Each of us, I suppose, has a mental image conjured up by the questions at hand. My image happens to be that of a Gary Larson cartoon. If you're not familiar with Gary Larson, he's the guy who draws "The Far Side." He drew this wonderful cartoon of a man who is obviously deceased, and he's standing outside the Pearly Gates with suitcase in hand; but there's a note pasted on the gate that says, "Moved to 231 Maple Street." I can just see some Aztec . . . or, excuse me, some Toltec Indian coming up this way, knocking on Cliff Palace and finding a note saying, "We've moved."

Now, rumor has it that Al Ortiz . . . and some of you may know Al Ortiz—he's a fine scholar who is a San Juan Pueblo Indian. Al Ortiz says the Anasazi moved to Española and are now running bingo parlors there. I live in Taos, not so far from Española, so I drove down to check out Al's claim. I asked three or four people I met on the street there . . . I said, "Are you an Anasazi?" And they said, "No." They shook their heads and pointed back *this* way, back toward Dolores. So here we are, back at square one, ready to debate the question.

Detail of "Mancos Black-on-White" bowl. Anasazi Heritage Center.

On a more serious note, anyone who has visited any of the Pueblo communities knows that the Anasazi are alive and well in their current locations, and that, in a real sense, they may be doing much better than the rest of us. One of the things that has impressed me so much about Pueblo culture is its durability. We could learn a lot from the Pueblos, particularly about the proper relationship between man and land. We, who currently change our culture given any whim emanating from either coast, could certainly do well to emulate the Pueblo people, who have managed to keep much of their Anasazi blood alive under the most adverse circumstances. That kind of tenacity is indeed enviable.

But let's get back to the subject at hand. As introduced, my name is Jim Judge, and I'm here to introduce this eminent panel and moderate their discourse. And, if appropriate, I may offer a view or two of my own. I hope, however, that that won't be necessary. I'm truly honored to be with these distinguished colleagues: Dave Breternitz, Linda Cordell, George Gumerman, Leigh Jenkins, Ed Ladd, and Bill Lipe.

Incidentally, and speaking archaeologically, the Four Corners area is very well represented here. Dave has done research in southwest Colorado; Linda, in New Mexico; George, in northeast Arizona; and Bill in southeast Utah. So the archaeologists here have covered the area geographically in terms of research interests, and certainly they all are very knowledgeable about the subject. Leigh Jenkins brings a personal perspective about the Anasazi from Hopi, and Ed Ladd brings a personal perspective from the pueblo of Zuni.

My own perspective is not . . . well, I'm neutral. I actually did my research on paleo-Indian, and then on Chaco. So I view the abandonment of the Four Corners area from the perspective of "those who came before" [earlier archaeologists], and not from the present. I could learn much from the discussion this evening.

What happened to the Anasazi? Where did they go? Why did they leave? These are the basic questions, but there are also others, and I'm sure that some of the other questions will be brought out as the discussion proceeds. For instance, *how* did the Anasazi leave? Was the abandonment that we now see—

through archaeology—perceptible to the individuals involved, or did it occur over several generations? Was it massive and quick? Perhaps more important, why didn't the Anasazi come back? A lot of people have visited Mesa Verde since the Anasazi left, so why didn't the Anasazi come back, let's say, in the fourteen and fifteen hundreds? And, then, why did they *all* leave, rather than just some of them? These are the questions that might come up and be examined tonight.

We'll ask each participant to speak individually on these matters, and then, I hope, we'll get a lot of audience involvement.

I'm going to go alphabetically. In terms of introducing the people, believe me—and you'll have to trust me on this—the credentials up here are so incredible that we would be here the rest of the evening if I just introduced people and told you how expert they were—or are. I'm going to proceed alphabetically in introducing them, and simply introduce them as friends and colleagues, people who are truly knowledgeable about the subject.

I'll begin with Dave Breternitz, who got his academic training at the University of Arizona. He now lives in Dove Creek, Colorado, and is a favorite here locally, I understand. He was also responsible for the Dolores Project, one of the largest federally sponsored archaeological projects ever undertaken.

Dave Breternitz
on *Theories of Abandonment*

So that we might have a general background, I am going to give a short basic review of ideas regarding abandonment of the Four Corners area that have been proposed previously. Basically, four reasons have been given for the abandonment of the Four Corners area by the Anasazi around A.D. 1300. First, and perhaps foremost, is *the drought of A.D. 1276 to A.D. 1299*. This climatic episode was proposed in the 1920s and '30s primarily through the work of A. E. Douglass and others who determined the existence of the "Great Drought" through the study of tree rings. Because the end of the Great Drought coincided with the abandonment of the general Anasazi area, it continues to be discussed as—if not *the* cause—a contributing factor.

A second reason that has been proposed is *arroyo cutting* [accelerated channel erosion]. This idea was proposed by a geologist, Kirk Bryan, about 1941, and was based primarily on work that he had conducted in Chaco Canyon. Arroyo cutting as a factor in abandonment applies [so Bryan believed] to the Chaco Canyon area, which was, as you probably know, unoccupied by A.D. 1300. Regardless, arroyo cutting is a second major reason that has been given for the overall abandonment of the Four Corners area. A "subset" of arroyo cutting is evidence of deforestation in some portions of the Anasazi area . . . deforestation would contribute to arroyo cutting.

Third, in 1936 Harold S. Colton came up with the idea of *epidemics, the "great disease theory,"* as it were. Based on studies that he did around Flagstaff, Arizona, Dr. Colton proposed that perhaps when people in the late 1200s got together and lived in closer contact, in larger sites . . . that due to the unsanitary conditions and this more intimate contact, the populations became highly susceptible to disease and epidemics. The disease explanation has not been accepted by scholars as *the* cause of abandonment of the Four Corners area, although it may have been a factor in some localities.

And then, fourth, there was *warfare*—enemy peoples or internal strife. This idea was probably first presented back in 1924 by A. V. Kidder in his *Introduction to the Study of Southwestern Archaeology*. Very recently, particularly in the Kayenta area, work carried on by Jonathan Haas has revived interest in this aspect of possible abandonment, at least for the Kayenta area. Although almost everyone knowledgeable about the prehistory of the Anasazi accepts the fact that there are many, many defensive, defensible, walled, and otherwise protected sites dating to the A.D. 1250–1300 time period, for some reason we are hesitant to recognize these sites as evidence of warfare.

In addition to these four primary reasons given for the Anasazi abandonment of the Four Corners area, there are a couple of other ideas that deserve mention. In 1951, William Y. Adams utilized data obtained on a survey in the Kayenta country and proposed the idea of the "Lure of the Bright Lights." The basic idea is that when crops failed . . . you ran short of potential marriage partners, and when things were going generally bad at home, you went to the "big city"; people congregated in larger sites where there were potential marriage partners, more social activities, and, perhaps, crop surpluses.

All the reasons for abandonment noted previously take into account the fact that during the A.D. 1250–1300 time period, the northern Anasazi were indeed moving into large, aggregated communities. And, let's face it, aggregation during time of stress is silly. Instead of *congregating* in times of stress, it makes more sense to spread out over the countryside. But we all realize that human beings do not always act in a rational manner. All we have to do is look at the Third World today—in places like Ethiopia and Mexico and Egypt. What do people do? They go to Addis Ababa and Mexico City and Cairo, and they are generally poorer and worse off than they were out where farming was stressful.

Yet another idea relating to abandonment of the Four Corners area was expressed by Emma Lou Davis, back in 1965, as "small pressures and cultural drift." Because that term more or less encompasses most of the ideas mentioned previously, it has appeal, but it is too non-specific to provide more than a framework for further data.

So, several ideas have been presented to explain why the Anasazi left the Four Corners, and there is still a lack of agreement, as we will see as this panel progresses.

I would also like to present a bit of information that is well documented but not well known at the present time, pertaining to the abandonment question. It concerns that which people do in times of stress, based on information from sites excavated during the Dolores Archaeological Project (DAP), between 1978 and 1985. Two persons who worked on the DAP, Sarah Schlanger and Richard Wilshusen, have continued to analyze the available data and have arrived at some interesting conclusions. In the Dolores River valley, which basically was occupied between A.D. 600 and 950, the prehistoric inhabitants abandoned the valley on four occasions for short periods of time. First of all, between A.D. 700 and 730, there is good evidence that nobody lived in the Dolores River valley—for that thirty-year period. Then the people came back for a short time, but during the decade A.D. 750 to 760 the valley appears again to have been devoid of inhabitants. They did return for about forty years, and then between A.D. 800 and 820 they left again—and then returned again to the valley. And then again they left, between A.D. 880 and 910.

So the pattern of abandoning local portions of the northern Southwest was practiced—at least in the Dolores valley—long before the final abandonment in about A.D. 1300. My question is this: If this practice of short-term abandonment of a small area repeatedly took place over time, why didn't this also happen about A.D. 1300? Why did the Anasazi *finally* leave? What was the straw that broke the camel's back? Why didn't they return one more time? I can only say that I know they weren't here during those four periods between A.D. 600 and 950.

Jim Judge

Thank you, Dave. Next in alphabetical order is Dr. Linda Cordell. Linda got her degree at the University of California, Santa Barbara, and she has worked extensively in New Mexico. And, I have to add, she is the author of the standard, now-adopted textbook in Southwest archaeology.

Linda Cordell
on *Anasazi Destinations in New Mexico*

I was asked to represent the New Mexico side of this, for having worked in New Mexico. And I figured that that was a pretty good deal, because at least we know—or those of us who have spent time in New Mexico know—that we can partially deal with the question of "where the Anasazi went." If anything, I would like to kind of convince you that we do know a little bit about that. And then perhaps I'll come back to talking about *why* they left, or why I think they left.

I was optimistic enough and foolish enough to have decided that I was going to do this as a slide show, not realizing, of course, that the sun was going to be out. So in a positive vein, if you lose me, I'll mime my slides for you and show you what they were all about.

In my set of slides I just wanted to convince you of something that Jim Judge has already spoken of. When one is standing at Mesa Verde and looking at the

Detail of "Mesa Verde Black-on-White" mug. Mesa Verde National Park.

beautiful cliff dwellings and the spectacular scenery and hearing the term "Anasazi" over and over, one gets this mystical feeling of some vanished people of long, long ago. And, of course, that's how publishers sell books. So they try to use those terms as well. And what that simply does is divorce the archaeological material that you're looking at from the Anasazi's contemporary "today" descendants, who are certainly the Pueblo Indians of Arizona and New Mexico. There is no doubt of that. There has not been any doubt of that for at least one hundred and some-odd years. And the glory of the slides was simply to show you that, yes indeed, the architecture is still pretty much the same, now as then. There are remarkable continuities in crafts. There are remarkable continuities in symbols that are painted on kiva walls—walls related to the prehistoric period—that show costumes that are still being worn. Some symbols are recognized by all Pueblo people.

We must not lose sight of the fact that "Anasazi" is a technical term invented by archaeologists to deal with all of this stuff, and that it [the term] bears little relationship to the people who were culturally, in fact, Pueblo people.

Having said that, I readily admit that archaeologists sometimes don't do as well, perhaps, as some other scholars because they're dealing with cultures which lack written languages. We do not have the written record of the folks up here who said, "Well, my wife and I had a fight on Thursday night, and I'm heading down to Santa Fe tomorrow, and maybe a few folks will go with me." We don't have that kind of thing. So therefore, when we talk about Anasazi, we're saying among other things that we're not sure what language they spoke.

We have no written record in that regard. We are not sure how the Anasazi identified themselves, or whether the people living in Chaco Canyon and those at Mesa Verde considered themselves totally different peoples—different tribal entities. We don't know. So we use labels to refer to the tangible kinds of things that archaeologists find. And those things are largely archaeological sites and the artifacts in them. Those things don't give you many direct notions as to how the Anasazi left.

Detail of "Mesa Verde Black-on-White" canteen. Anasazi Heritage Center.

In terms of where they went, I would like to comment that they went to an area that extended on the east to Pecos, New Mexico, and certainly to the Hopi mesas in the west. Since I'm only dealing with New Mexico, I have not covered the Hopi population and the Hopi mesas. But I thought it would be nice to give you some figures.

This [the immediate Four Corners area] is the archaeological center of the Anasazi universe. This is, as I phrase it, downtown Anasazi here. You've got lots of archaeological sites. But so do we down farther south and farther east.

So let's look at some very recent and excellent data from work that was done on the Pajarito Plateau in New Mexico by the University of California, Los Angeles, directed by Dr. James Hill. They have discovered that at one time, shortly after A.D. 1270, there were 142 sites having mean ground floor areas of 175 square meters. Somewhat later, there were seventy-seven sites with 387 mean square meters of ground floor space. And then, finally, forty-three sites . . . but now these are much larger, with 899 square meters of ground floor space. Instantly I know you see pictures in your mind of these sites. Well, I was going to show you slides of them. But, you know what? The slides aren't very good anyway. How many unexcavated archaeological sites look wonderful in pictures? "All right, there's another blob of bushes." You know, the sites are under a big blob of bushes. But those are a lot of sites, and they're big sites.

The Galisteo Basin, which is also in that area . . . it's sort of Shirley MacLaine country. It's southeast of Santa Fe. We have really big sites there. We have Pueblo Largo. That's a small one, the smallest one, with 489 ground floor rooms. Pueblo Colorado has 881 ground floor rooms, and we don't know how many other floors as well. They could have gone up [built upward]. Pueblo She' has 1,543 ground floor rooms. That's bigger than Pueblo Bonito, bigger than Chetro Ketl. Pueblo Blanco has 1,450 ground floor rooms, and San Lázaro 1,900 ground floor rooms. These are late prehistoric sites and they were occupied presumably after *this* area [the immediate Four Corners] was abandoned, but before the historic period.

I will also comment on some of the written record that's available, to let you

know that not all 1,400 and some-odd rooms [of Pueblo Blanco] were occupied at the same time. We seem to have horizontal shifting of people within the site, but these are very large sites. The largest adobe ruin in New Mexico is Sapawe . . . it covers some sixty-nine acres. That's a *big* site. Howiri Ruin, again in the Chama country, has 500 rooms, and Tsiping has 300 rooms.

Probably the more spectacular are the Zuni pueblos, which Ed Ladd will probably elaborate on. Near Zuni there are several large sites that date to the period between A.D. 1250 and 1300. In fact, there are twelve sites around Zuni that each has more than 400 rooms, and two of those have more than 700 rooms, and two others more than 1,000 rooms.

A little bit later, there are *nineteen* sites with more than 400 rooms, and nine of those have 700 rooms or more.

So I think we can say that, for whatever reasons the Anasazi left *here*, they certainly wound up in the areas that I have indicated, as well as farther west, to the Hopi area. And I think we can tell this by, really, two things. One is the presence of the very large sites, and the other is the fact that through time the sites became more aggregated. In other words, some individual sites became larger, and some other sites were abandoned.

I think that—although I agree completely with Dave Breternitz in his comments that in adversity most people do not aggregate, rather they split if they possibly can—I couldn't agree more—but I think in other circumstances, where they cannot split because there are people surrounding them who will not easily give them living room, that indeed you get aggregation.

I would also like to comment that, even though we can talk about continuity of all kinds, when we look at pueblos as being where they are for countless centuries—and I mean right where they are, like Zuni right where it is or Santo Domingo right where it is—that, in fact, we're looking at a problem of these people not necessarily being able to move, because they are controlled by an outside government right now that says this is the "res" [reservation], and also because they're surrounded by other peoples. I'm not sure that we aren't looking,

Detail of "Chaco Black-on-White" pitcher. Museum of the American Indian, Heye Foundation.

perhaps, past a very long-term pattern of somewhat more residential mobility.

Having said that, I will address, sort of, the four explanations that have been given, and some of the sidelights, too. Because I think that's fun. I think we should take a vote afterwards . . . "How many think the Great Drought? or . . .".

The *Great Drought*. Well, the Great Drought was only one of several droughts. I know that because I did my doctoral dissertation using climate data from Mesa Verde to predict when things got bad and when people might leave. And I did a lot of looking at various periods of drought, and indeed the Great Drought was a great drought. But there were others before. I think people [archaeologists] today would comment simply that the Great Drought toward the end of things also coincided with a very dense population for the area . . . in which there were few alternatives. Try living in the area for that long. It's hard to go back to being a hunter and gatherer when you've hunted and gathered everything edible in the vicinity, and your mobility is constrained by the people around you.

Arroyo cutting. Sure, that's possible. But these folks were excellent farmers, and they still are. They knew lots and lots of ways of preventing erosion. So I'm not totally convinced.

Disease. Sure, that might have been a factor. Unfortunately, epidemic diseases, as Colton suggested, are among those that do not normally leave any sort of physical evidence that's observable on skeletons. And we do not, in fact, have things that look like the mass graves of people who have died in an epidemic.

Warfare. I've been accused of being anti-warfare. I am in present political circumstances. Warfare seems to be the thing, you know, that haunts a lot of people, that comes up over and over again. I just want to point out that one of my graduate students, who is very much enamored of the warfare idea, decided to demonstrate that warfare was the key. And what he did was go back over everybody's work in the Southwest who had mentioned warfare once or twice; and his term paper, which was the most honest piece of work I have ever received, basically found that the only correlation he could get with warfare were the dates of publication, which coincided either with when the United States was about to enter a war or was in the midst of one. Okay. I don't deny that it's a possibility.

When we look at the regional abandonment, part one is to say what period. It was regional. Yes, if we look at Dolores and some of these other places, we look at ins and outs. In fact, there's a reason to suspect that the Anasazi were not firmly committed to a place. But, on the other hand, sometime between 1150 and 1300 a whole lot of this area was abandoned. That's a major *regional* phenomenon. And I think that suggests to me, as it has to others on the panel, that the region was somewhat integrated prehistorically. The fact that maybe the center fell out of Chaco at one point means that it was harder for everybody else. The old network was gone.

My doctoral advisor once explained the Dark Ages on the basis of the fact that the Arabs had disrupted trade routes between Asia and Europe. So this is a possibility.

In looking at Chaco, though, and abandonment, I have to come back to asking my colleague, Jim Judge—and I hope he will tell me—how many people are we looking at who left? Because the counts from there vary from, I think, about 1,000 or so, individuals, to 10,000. I can't know the magnitude of the system that collapsed or where they went without having some idea of how many folks were there. If there were only eleven people who left, we don't have a lot to worry about.

But at any rate, I do think that there is an interrelated factor. And I would comment—to throw in one of my own ideas, and it's original to me—that . . . I think some Navajo people have a good story about it . . . it [prehistoric Chaco life] had gotten too far away from things. It was too abstract, as the Navajo say. Chaco was too involved in something that had nothing to do with the land. It was too political; it was too strange. It was a system that was very rigorous, but it didn't quite work to balance the natural problems that [can] occur in an agriculturally marginal area. So when it was gone, perhaps the peripheries that were up *here* and densely inhabited could no longer maintain themselves in place. Then what did they do? They went down and joined—as I think Dave has said accurately—the "bright lights." Not because of the bright lights, but because there were folks "making it" elsewhere. In the Zuni area, the Pajarito Plateau, the Galisteo Basin, and the Hopi area, there were people in place who provided them entree.

Anyway, you can question that, or anything else, but that's my scenario for now.

Jim Judge

Thank you very much, Linda. George Gumerman is next. George has his degree from the University of Arizona, and he worked for many years in the Black Mesa Project in northeast Arizona.

George Gumerman
on *Variations in Anasazi Society*

First, I would like to thank the Bureau of Land Management for hosting this event, and also I would thank you, the audience. Ten years ago we would have been sitting talking to ourselves, without benefit of trying to spread what we know to interested people or to get feedback from them. So, thanks to the BLM and to you.

This carnival atmosphere in archaeology—and it's not just the tent we are in, but the sideshows that are going on here [at the "Four Corners Tribute"]—is truly a marvelous thing for archaeology. And it's about time we started doing some of these things for the general public, because, after all, you are the people who are paying for the archaeology that we're doing.

Now, I would like to say that, in my view, there is no mystery about where the Anasazi went. I don't think the Anasazi are unusual. If we look at other, similar, simple agricultural societies, we see the same trajectory that we see with the Anasazi. Even looking just at the Southwest—at the Hohokam of southern Arizona and at the Mogollon of the mountainous areas of Arizona and New Mexico—all of whom, along with the Anasazi, became dependent upon agriculture at about the same time—we see similar processes happening. Increases in population, the development of social complexity, specialists developing—we see small communities, very small communities, becoming large towns with impressive architecture; and we see some areas being abandoned. But we see people moving into bigger centers. And we see certain areas that become "hot spots," developing more rapidly than other places. These hot spots cool down after a while and other areas seem to take the cultural evolutionary lead.

If you look at the eastern United States, after the advent of agriculture you see the same process going on. What we see is similar to other parts of the world. So what we see with the Anasazi I don't think is that unusual.

Now, one of the wonderful things about southwestern archaeology is that we have so much information, perhaps more detail than for any other area of the world. And this is in terms of data about the people and in terms of things like tree-ring dating and climatic reconstruction. We have a tremendous amount of information which has resulted from an incredible amount of effort in doing the archaeology in the Southwest. In fact, my former colleague, Shirley Powell, who is here today, said at one time when we were working at Black Mesa that she thought there were probably more archaeologists working at Black Mesa than there ever were Anasazi. The data for all this work has allowed us the luxury of testing our ideas.

What is interesting to most archaeologists is the big-picture kind of question, like, "What happened to the Anasazi? Why did they move? Where did they go?" And the interesting thing is that we have now a tension between these big-picture kinds of question about the Anasazi and the incredibly detailed information that we have about small local regions. It is this tension between the big questions we are asking and the data from local areas that allows us to look at the incredible variation that was going on in Anasazi [in the Anasazi area at the time(s) of abandonment].

As Linda has pointed out, we call them all Anasazi. But we don't know how they divided themselves into various groups. We can, however, see an incredible amount of varying behavior—valley to valley, mesa to mesa, these people were not behaving in the same ways; they reacted differently to similar situations.

What I had wanted to do was compare a very parochial, down-home kind of place, Black Mesa in northern Arizona. . . . In twenty years there we didn't find a single piece of turquoise. If there were railroad tracks in Anasazi land, the Black Mesa people were on the wrong side of them. What I wanted to do briefly was compare the people on Black Mesa—how they changed, how they adapted to stress—compare that to Chaco Canyon. But all of my colleagues up here said, "No, you'll go on and on and on, and bore everybody, including us. And we won't put up with it." So you'll have to wait for some other time.

But the interesting thing to me is that there was a suite of things which affected change. And I think the question perhaps could most interestingly be focused by asking not, "What happened to the Anasazi, where did they go and why did they go?" but a more general question: "How did the Anasazi society change and why did it change?" The question is important because we, as anthropologists, are interested in all forms of change.

I personally felt for many years that there was an environmental reason for much of Anasazi change, but not simply rainfall. Groundwater supplies and erosion, arroyo cutting, the topography of the landscape, how the resources such as the piñon trees and the clay for ceramics are scattered over the landscape . . . such things have all had an impact on Anasazi stability and change.

Of equal importance is the character of the social organization in each locale, which allows people to respond in certain ways, or *not* respond in certain ways, to the stress of other groups coming into the territory . . . or to environmental degradation, precipitation decline, erosion, or a drop in groundwater. How individual Anasazi communities were organized was very important; it determined how they could or could not respond. A contemporary example is the oil crisis in the 1970s. It hit California much worse than it did people living in Manhattan because California people depend on family cars, while New Yorkers depend on mass transportation. I think it is vital to understand how the individual Anasazi communities were organized to determine how they reacted to various kinds of stress.

Detail of "Mesa Verde Black-on-White" bowl. From Mug House, Mesa Verde National Park.

For example, Chaco Canyon started to collapse after a series of years when summer rainfall was in decline. Other areas lasted longer. The more simply organized societies, ones that were spread out over the landscape and that depended more on hunting and the gathering of wild seeds, were not affected as much by drought as were those societies that relied on agriculture. I'm thinking about the places north of Winslow and Holbrook called the Hopi Buttes, that lasted for another century [after the Chaco collapse], until things got much worse. And yet they were a much less complex society than Chaco. So I think that how a society is organized has a lot to do with how it can react to various kinds of stress.

What this means is *decision making*, and the previous speakers have talked about this. We have an archaeological colleague at the University of New Mexico famous for saying, "We are poorly equipped, as archaeologists, to be paleopsychologists." Okay. And yet, at the same time, when a group *decides* to move, there are all sorts of cultural baggage that affect the decision to move. Maybe we're all poorly equipped to be paleopsychologists, but we need some insight into how decisions are made. Is there a clan system in the society? If there is a clan system, that may make it easier for groups to move, because they have a set place in another community with their clan brethren. If there is no clan system, maybe the decision to move is more difficult. So the social-organizational aspect, I think, is very important in understanding what permits people to make decisions.

Now, is there something that we can call the essence of Anasazi? What makes an Anasazi? In talking about the big picture, we want to know [the answers to] these questions about the Anasazi and how they changed, and yet, we're also interested in the very localized behavior of Anasazi. Is there something that makes these local groups of people with different kinds of behavior something we can call Anasazi? Well, I'm going to say something that is somewhat heretical to my professional colleagues.

We have preached for years now that the essence of archaeology is to understand human behavior, to understand change and stability—why things change and why they don't change. And I still think that's true. But because we see such incredible variation in Anasazi behavior—how they behaved, how they used kivas, how they made a living from the environment—it is difficult to characterize Anasazi behavior in general. Maybe the essence of Anasazi for our purpose is some things like black-on-white pottery, corrugated or plain grayware pottery, fine masonry construction, features in the ground that we call kivas. Maybe artifacts and architecture are the essence of Anasazi. I say that because I'm trying to emphasize that we see a great deal of variation from area to area within the Anasazi region.

The things that we see that are similar are these common markers in the archaeological records, such as black-on-white pottery.

So, with that somewhat heretical statement, I'll go back to Jim.

Jim Judge

Again, proceeding alphabetically here, the next speaker is Leigh Jenkins, who is the Hopi Tribe's cultural preservation officer, and who is here this week participating in the Four Corners Governors Conference.

Leigh Jenkins on *The Hopi View*

I guess if you hang around until Thursday, you'll probably find the answers to the questions being posed here, because probably around six o'clock, the Anasazi will go home to Hopiland. And this Anasazi will even tell you what he went with, probably a 1986 Chevy Celebrity.

Anyway, with that, I'll go into my comments, offering, I hope, a different perspective on some of the questions that are being talked about here today during the forum.

My name is Leigh Jenkins, and I'm the tribe's cultural preservation officer. And during the one and a half years that I've held this position I've had an opportunity to really study *archaeologists*. For me it's quite refreshing to begin to hear some thought that adds a little further substance to some of the hypotheses that, of course, people have to work around in making some kind of conclusions. What I'd like to do, really, is talk about one facet of work that we're engaged in at Hopi. And that is: we're trying to organize some very specific ethno-historic and ethnology-type projects.

One of the things that disturbs me very much—and I really, of course, continue to raise my eyebrows—is hearing some of these very questions continually asked. Because we feel strongly, from the Hopi side, that the Anasazi, as well as other Puebloan-classified cultures—like the Fremont farther north, and the Sinagua near Flagstaff—are in fact ancestral Hopi people. And not much credence is ever lent, I believe, to some of the ways that Indian people have preserved their history.

In Hopi there are a number of things that I feel demonstrate and validate the Hopi claim to aboriginal presence here in the Four Corners area. One thing that's very simple—but I think very important to the Hopi way of interpreting the presence of ancestral Hopis here in this area—is the interpretation of rock art. The minute I walked into the Anasazi Heritage Center here, the first things that caught my eye were some of the rock art panels depicted in photographs. Some of the clan symbols I readily identify.

You know, my clan, which is now the Third Mesa Clan—the Greasewood Clan—traveled these lands with the Bow Clan, the Reed Clan, and the Roadrunner Clan. Our clan, the Greasewood Clan, is today in Hopi alluded to primarily as "Utes." I mean, it's because we stayed for a long, long time around these areas and subsequently had an influx of some of the Ute people from farther north. We consequently achieved a lot of social affiliation with those people. And when we finally arrived back on the mesas of Hopi, we carried some of the knowledge of the Ute people. And to this day the people of my clan, the Greasewood Clan, are noted for that affiliation with the Ute people.

You know, oral history is very special to me. In my forty years of growing up on the Hopi, we go through a process of, I suppose, earning our doctorate. And that's through the process of initiations into different ceremonies and societies, where you begin to get more privileged information shared by some of the elders. We begin to learn symbols. We begin to learn the meaning of color, different types of color, direction color, what color signifies to Hopi. And suddenly you begin to understand what Hopi history is all about.

And, of course, I would prefer that you know the Hopi word *Hisatsinom*, to the Navajo word *Anasazi*. And that's just a personal comment there. That's really

Detail of "Tusayan White Ware" potsherd. From Black Mesa, Arizona.

the name of these people who traveled many, many parts of the Southwest that we know as the Four Corners region today. *Hisatsinom* literally means "people of long ago." But to the Hopi . . . they are the ancestors of the Hopi. Today we carry on some of the very traditions and ceremonies that our clan and our ancestors carried on during their migrations.

In 1966 among various scholars, when the first real publication that collaborated with Hopi authorities came out—and that was the *Book of the Hopi*—there was this big debate that supposedly the Germans were somehow related to the Hopi because of the swastika. So there was this big debate. You know, the swastika is merely a migration symbol. It is a symbol of the four directional routes, the cardinal directions that Hopis were spiritually mandated to set their footprints on. The spiritual mandate also talked about why there was the need to do that . . . and that need was to proclaim on behalf of the great spirit the stewardship over these lands. So the sights that you see, and some of the shards that are scattered throughout the Southwest, were only testimony to the presence of the Hopi ancestral people. They are monuments and hallmarks that attest, in fact, that Hopi people, through their clans, like my clan, stayed around these lands for periods of time.

One only needs to go to Hopi and talk to a Hopi to learn why the Navajo National Monument area, in which there are numerous ruins, was suddenly abandoned. And the Hopi will merely tell you, "Well, if you want to know, I'll talk to you about why." The Hopis have a Navajo kachina. And they'll tell you the whole story.

So I guess from that perspective really, I guess . . . I am expressing my appreciation that at least some recognition is beginning to come to the oral history of different cultural groups, including the Hopi people. Because the Anasazi didn't go anywhere. We're still around.

So, with that, I'd like to extend my appreciation to the BLM—and certainly to the panel here—for allowing me to be a part of this presentation. And I certainly am available for debate. Thank you.

Jim Judge

Thank you very much, Leigh. The next speaker is Ed Ladd. Ed had a long and illustrious career in the National Park Service. And he is also attending the Four Corners Governors Conference here. Ed is going to bring us the words and wisdom of the Zuni Tribe.

Ed Ladd
on *The Zuni View*

I'm going to stand up, too, because I can't sit talking. [*Mr. Ladd then speaks in his native tongue for a few moments*] I just thought I'd like to say something in Zuni.

In the very beginning, the very beginning of time, there were no humans in this world. Sun Father came up in the east, he came up and went over the mountains, over the sea, rested at high noon for a spell, and descended to the west and went into the western ocean, and night fell. All night long, all night long Sun Father traveled under the earth, and he traveled until he came to the east again to bring a new day. But the new day was not filled with joy, the new day was not filled with laughter. All he could hear was cries of his children in Mother Earth's womb. So he created these twin war gods, the Twin Gods. And he said unto them, "Go and bring my children up in my light." And so they did. But the origin was one that was many faceted. They moved up from the lower earth below, and they started moving. They moved every four years, and in all directions. . . .

If you can take a look at the "measles map" you'll see why. Of course, there are a lot of Anasazi ruins. They're scattered all over the place because that's where our ancestors traveled. They weren't traveling because there were droughts or there was pestilence. They were traveling because they were looking, searching, for the center place. Each one, until they found their own center place, moved every four years. Actually they said every four days, but they actually meant four years. And they moved in any direction, any direction, with all kinds of languages. [Editor's note: The "measles map" mentioned by Mr. Ladd is an unpublished map of the Four Corners area, with red dots indicating locations of Anasazi sites having fifty or more rooms each. The sites were identified and plotted on the map during a March 1990 conference at Crow Canyon Archaeological Center, Cortez, Colorado.

Detail of "Mesa Verde Black-on-White" bowl. From Mug House, Mesa Verde National Park.

The sites on the "measles map" were occupied between A.D. 1150 and 1350.]

Of course we know where we came from. Of course we know why we call ourselves *A:shiwi*. I can remember my little nephew and all of the Anglos who said, "Look at the cute little Indian, look at the cute little Indian." And he would stand up to his full four-foot height and say, "I'm not an Indian. I'm a Zuni." So we don't really need to go searching the archaeological records. We don't really need to, that is, from our point of view.

And it's interesting that the archaeological answers are almost the same: "Well, they moved because. . . . " But the answers are more varying: "They moved because they were hungry, they moved because they were thirsty, because water ran out."

But *we* know why they moved. Because they were looking for the center place. And when they found the center place, that's where they settled. That's where Zuni is now today. That's where Hopi is. That's where Ácoma is. That's where San Ildefonso is. That's where Santo Domingo is. And these are the Anasazi. They moved from the San Juan River basin areas and settled into the modern-day pueblos. They already have a name for themselves. The Hopis have a name for themselves. The Ácomas have a name for themselves. We don't call ourselves Anasazi because, as Jenkins says, *Anasazi* is a Navajo word. We would rather call our ancestors *Enote:que*, "our ancient ones, our ancestors." We would much rather call them that than Anasazi.

But as Jim says and Linda Cordell says, and others have said here, the archaeologists have coined this word *Anasazi* to mean the ancient ones. The translation is "the ancient ones." They occupied the whole of the San Juan River basin.

And, as I said before, we don't know what language they spoke. Interestingly enough, when you go to Zuni, Zuni is the only place you can speak Zuni, because there is no other language related to the Zuni. And maybe they are the original Anasazi, I don't know. Or, they could have been the original Mogollon or the Hohokam. Again, all are anthropologically coined words. We still call ourselves *A:shiwi*. I am *Shiwi*, and my people are the *A:shiwi*.

Now, you've heard the white man's myth and story of the origin of people, people moving from one place to another because of hunger. We know why they moved and we know where they originated. Some of them came from the streams and the rivers to the north. Some of them came up the rivers north to the Rio Grande. Some of them came up from the rivers in the Grand Canyon.

And so many other places are sacred to us because we moved through this country, through this whole country. Our religion is not just . . . it's a day-to-day religion. It's every day and every hour of every day that is religious for us. The spirits that occupy the springs, the mountaintops, the four oceans that surround us are . . . all are places where the spirits live, and we share these places with them. And what you can't seem to understand is the fact that our world and our universe is limitless. We say, in metaphorical terms, "From the four corners of the world, to the four corners surrounding the world, to the moss-covered mountains and the oceans, our world is our temple." And anytime you harm . . . these are not sacred places, but these are respected and venerated places where the spirits live. And we share this land with the spirits.

And so when you talk about Anasazi, think about the people that are living today in the Rio Grande valley, and about the Zunis and the Ácomas and the Hopis, because that's where they are. Different, slightly different, yes, but still the same. And, with that, I'll close.

Jim Judge

Thank you very much, Ed. The last participant, last speaker, is Bill Lipe. Bill got his academic training at Yale, worked in southeast Utah, and now is very closely connected with the Crow Canyon Archaeological Center.

Bill Lipe
on *Some Attractions to the South*

One of the good things about being last on a podium like this is that you get a chance to hear what everyone else had to say, and to criticize them and so forth. One of the bad things, of course, is that people are still waiting for an answer to the questions that we started with. I'll do what I can.

I think we've done a lot better in understanding *where* the Anasazi went and who they are now, than in understanding *why* they left this Four Corners area, and why they left when and how they did.

I must say that the accounts of Leigh and Ed are hard to refute. Those are accounts that have been passed down for a long time. As Ed pointed out, the accounts you get from the anthropologists come out of a different tradition, a tradition that is basically a scientific one, or at least a historical one. And it's one in which a *certainty,* such as the Indian accounts convey about human origins, really isn't established. [In the scientific tradition] *certainty* really isn't the point.

That brings me back to the problem of getting a real answer to this question, considered in the way of thinking that we do in anthropology. I think generally that in history and science as practiced in Western civilization we don't come to final conclusions. We try to evaluate alternative accounts. So I think the best we can do with this [question of Anasazi exodus] . . . well, we can't, from that perspective, dispose of it with a final answer. But perhaps we can evaluate some of these accounts. And I think we've done some of that.

Having said that, I'll give my view, from an anthropological perspective, of what I think might have been going on with the Anasazi. And I'll make a few comments about how parts of what went on might be consistent with the accounts that come to us from the older Pueblo tradition.

I brought this map, which Ed called the "measles map." [*Dr. Lipe directs the attention of the audience to a display-size map*] The state boundaries are on it not because they have any relevance to the problem, but just to give an orientation. Here we are . . . this is the Montezuma valley right here, and this is Phoenix down here. The red dots show the Puebloan sites of fifty or more rooms, all of which we were able to plot in a conference that we had at Crow Canyon in March [1990]. These sites were occupied at some time in the period 1150 to 1350, which is basically the period when the Anasazi bailed out of the Four Corners country. I'd just like to use this map to put the entire matter into geographic perspective.

[*Pointing to the map*] This is the largest extent of the Puebloan area, this huge area where these red dots are. Pueblos were being built here during that 1150-

to-1350 period. Here is the area that the Anasazi bailed out of. It's the northern part of the Pueblo area, but it's not the largest or most prominent part of the entire Pueblo area. It's just the northern part of it. Actually, you can say that during this period the Pueblo people expanded their territory. They did bail out of the north, but they established a heck of a lot of new settlements and joined and added to existing settlements farther south.

And then there's a further contraction later on, in the late 1300s and 1400s, from the *south*, with the people contracting into some of the areas that are still occupied today. And that latter contraction raises a question as interesting as the one, "why did they leave the north?" or the one "why did they contract their range from the north and expand their range in the south during this period?" But, fortunately, I don't have to address this later southern contraction.

Let me just say a few things about some of the ideas that . . . I really don't think I have any new ideas here, but I'd like to look at the "why" part of the problem—why this particular area may have been abandoned when it was. It seems to me that you can make a case that climate had something to do with it. I don't think you can make a case that climate pushed *everybody* out. But climate may have made this area unstable at the time. That is, I think you can make a case from the tree-ring record, the geological record, and the pollen record, and so forth, that there may have been kind of a climatic "squeeze play" going on here. I know these people were good farmers, and they had excellent abilities, they had good lands, and so forth. But I think there may have been, in the late 1100s and 1200s, some conjunction of factors that may have put a squeeze on at least some of the people in this area. There were some recurrent droughts, particularly in the late 1100s, but also in the 1200s, that would have affected their intermediate-elevation dry farming. There are also some pollen and tree-ring records—and this is shakier—that indicate there might have been some cooling trends that possibly affected some higher-elevation agriculture. There is also evidence of some arroyo cutting that may have affected agriculture in the valleys and floodplains. So both the dry-farming areas and the floodplain-farming areas

Detail of "Mesa Verde Black-on-White" mug. Mesa Verde National Park.

would have been hurt. But, I don't think that that conjunction of factors was enough to have pushed *everyone* out of this area.

However, it may have created a situation in which some other alternatives looked more attractive.

At the same time that this was happening—the late 1100s and 1200s—there was growth in the Pueblo communities farther south. And I think there may also have been some *changes* in Pueblo communities farther south, some social and perhaps religious changes that may have been attractive to people up here in the Four Corners, who were under some kind of stress or some kind of unsettled conditions. I'm not sure of the precise timing of that, but it's close. However, the timing *is* critical.

One of the things we see in the south is a change in the older pattern of numerous kivas, one kiva for every ten or twelve rooms. Presumably a kiva was possessed at that time by a relatively small group, perhaps an extended family. That tends to change, starting in the south, to communities having fewer kivas—just as we see in the historic and modern periods—relatively few kivas per community. We also see a shift to larger communities and to plaza-oriented communities. It's possible that what we may be seeing is the development of new social organization and new religious systems in this southern area. These new systems may have been oriented toward stronger communities, whereas the older systems here in the north may have been more oriented to family levels, with decision making at the community level a lot weaker. I don't know. That's really speculation at this point.

If, however, some of these changes were taking place, say, in the early and middle 1200s—changes toward stronger communities, toward plaza orientations, toward kivas that perhaps belonged to religious societies rather than to families . . . well, perhaps those kinds of organization may have been attractive to people here in the Four Corners, people who were having some difficulty, though perhaps not to the point of being forced out.

A change in religious belief, or the idea of joining communities that had a new way or a new direction, might possibly have been attractive at this point. That seems to me the only way you could account for the rapid and complete abandonment of this area. I don't think the environmental evidence is enough to show that they were *forced* out in a hurry. But perhaps some kind of social or religious movement may have been enough to attract people who were already under stress, and some of whom were on the margin. So that's my speculation.

I think we need to take a longer look at that kind of idea, and look at it in terms of this whole system, not just in terms of the northern area. So I guess it's . . . you might call this a version of the "bright lights" theory. But maybe it's one that is a little further developed than just the notion of moving to larger settlements.

I guess, rather than putting much confidence in that specific reconstruction, I would say that we need to get beyond just looking at environmental change that might have *pushed* people out of here. We need to begin looking at social organization, and particularly at religious organization—which is today so central to Pueblo societies—as something that may have had an effect. Whether it's the way I've reconstructed it, I'm not sure. It's a matter that I'm playing with as a result of having tried to look at this whole pattern during this conference in March.

I could also say in closing, however, that some of the things we've heard tonight make me see, I think for the first time, the compatibility of the older, traditional accounts from Hopi and Zuni with some of the things that archaeologists have been finding out. It may be that ultimately archaeologists will come around to accepting those ideas, or at least to making them more compatible with the way they tend to look at things.

One of the things that we've heard here repeatedly from the archaeologists is that movement is a well-established pattern, movement from small scale to large scale. That is certainly compatible with the legends from the Indian traditions, of people searching for the center, or moving frequently.

We've also heard that probably there was a lot of land here, there was a lot of farmland in the Southwest. If people were able to colonize here and there over this huge area, it was a big niche, it was a big agricultural area. Even though there were lots of people, they could have lived a lot of places. This tends to weaken the "environmental push" kinds of theories. If there are lots of places that people could live, then perhaps the theories, including the one I've just given you, that show the Puebloans being pushed around by little climatic changes . . . maybe we need to take a really critical look at those theories. If it is a big area and people could live equally well in many parts of it, then maybe a belief that people had to keep moving and look for the right place could very well result in some of the patterns of movement we see in the archaeological record.

So those are some thoughts that occur to me. Again, I don't think that we've come up with any final answers, but perhaps we've strengthened some notions here and maybe gotten rid of, or put to the side, some other notions.

And certainly, speaking for myself and I hope for other people, I've learned a lot from this exercise. I thank you for making it possible.

Jim Judge

Ed Ladd would like just a couple of seconds more.

Ed Ladd

I think if you look at this pattern and system we're looking at . . . they [the Anasazi] could look at the system . . . and I've tried to understand it. I work with it. And I acknowledge the fact that this is an important facet of the system that we're working with. It's important that we understand the system and work hard with it, and get an understanding of the intricacies of the universe and the system itself.

Do you understand what I am saying? If you do, then we're in big trouble. Because that's the way archaeologists have been talking to us for years. We don't understand a lot of the gibberish that they're telling us. As the public, we're the ones paying for the archaeologists. But do you understand what they're talking about?

Yet I would like to say that one of the most interesting things about "movement" is the fact that my tribe is made up of a number of different facets, including religious societies that are not of Zuni origin. Rather, some things at Zuni had origins from other cultures in other areas. And I don't think the Anasazi all decided to bring down the curtain on Friday afternoon, to put their little packs on their backs and go to Zuni. I think there were movements in small numbers, movements of small numbers of people from one area to another for reasons other than drought, hunger, or whatever.

I think the social reasons and the religious reasons are a very important point. The number of kivas really is not significant, except the fact that there are large numbers in some areas. Even today Hopi has a proliferation of kivas. Zuni has six. The Rio Grande Pueblos have two. They have a moiety system [an organization of the people into two groups]; the Rio Grande Pueblos differ from any other system. So kivas are not necessarily an indication of a *lack* of either religious dissension or religious development, nor do they indicate a *proliferation* of either religous dissension or development. Why does Zuni have six and Hopi have . . . how many? . . . fourteen, fifteen, whatever? I don't know why they have them, but that's the way it is. And I know the Rio Grande Pueblos have moiety systems and two kivas, and that ours [at Zuni] is not a clan system. I detest the fact that everybody refers to these as "clan kivas." I don't think there's any such thing as a clan kiva. I think the kivas were utilized by extended family groups that were not necessarily clan units but units that cut across clans. Probably two or three extended family units would use one kiva. And I think that probably because of religious dissension they moved from one place to another. But they didn't all move en masse.

We have religious songs [at Zuni] that are from the Pima people of the Phoenix area and the lower valley areas. We have Navajo songs from the Navajo culture, and we have Rio Grande songs from the Rio Grande people. All are combined into a Zuni form. So I don't think this business of movement was such a great adventure. I don't see the Anasazi people moving en masse, going from one area to another. I see people moving in small numbers, moving from one area to another, and finally abandoning an area completely.

The fact that they sealed up some of the doorways would indicate to me that they hoped to come back one day. But they never did. They stayed where they went, to the "bright lights." Thank you.

Jim Judge

Thank you, Ed.

I would like to open the discussion to public participation now. I'm not going to give you my views, because I think the views of the public should be given a chance. But I'll say just one thing about my bias, and that is, I side with George Gumerman. In fact, I'm more radical than George. My environmental viewpoint, however, stems from two factors. One factor is, I was raised in Jackson Hole, Wyoming, where they get six feet of snow every year—and I moved out. The reason was environmental, and environmental only. The other reason is that George and I, between the two of us, outweigh the rest of the panel, and I think we could take them two out of three falls.

I'll open it up now for participation from you, the audience. If you have questions, I would like to entertain them. If you can, and if you feel free, please go use the microphone in the middle of the audience there. And I will reiterate your question, if need be, so that all can hear it; and I'll also direct it to the appropriate person to answer.

So are there any questions? Oh, and when you approach, or when you get to the microphone, please identify yourself.

Detail of "Mesa Verde Black-on-White" mug. Mesa Verde National Park.

Questions from the Audience

On the Future of the Anasazi/Pueblo People

AUDIENCE: I'm the archaeologist here at the Anasazi Heritage Center, Victoria Atkins. I've got a question I would like . . . it's a little more geared toward the future of the *Hisatsinom*—the Zuni . . . or Pueblo people. I would like to maybe address it to Leigh and Ed, particularly.

I think Jim made an excellent point about his admiration for the people who came before us, about their durability and their success as agriculturists. Some of you made the point that in the marginal areas they really stuck to it. And Mr. Jenkins was telling me this afternoon about his experience as a farmer today, about being one of the few farmers of his generation at the Hopi Reservation. Dr. Cordell mentioned that, although there's been a lot of movement in the past, one of the things that might be changing now [for the Pueblos] is the lack of an ability to move. There's no more frontier for a lot of people.

Therefore, I guess I'd just like to ask you, what do you think the future is? Do you think there are ways to succeed? And how can we help, as partners, for the future of the Hopi and the Zuni and the Rio Grande Pueblos, and lots of Native American groups that are starting to perhaps have a lot of pressure and perhaps a loss of culture and language and traditions? Thank you.

Detail of "Mancos Black-on-White" bowl. Anasazi Heritage Center.

JIM JUDGE: Leigh, would you like to comment on that?

LEIGH JENKINS: I guess what I'll do for an answer is to share with you a short little story: When the Hopi people emerged, and the guardian spirit came upon them, our stories say that the only material possessions that the spirit had were a planting stick, a patch of corn, and a jug of water. And I guess that's really the message that Hopi brings to everyone, that if there is yet a chance for all of us, it should be through the recognition of some of the basic elements of life in general.

You know, the great spirit laid out a life plan for the Hopi people, and we began to travel on that life plan. He stopped us short and said, "You also have your life plan." And it is so evident that we are now faced with a multitude of social problems that stem from basic human characteristics that we all have, such as greed, hunger for power, all those kinds of things that make our lives so much more difficult. I guess that's why in the Anasazi culture—that you see around here—you have just a very real demonstration of agricultural lifeways.

Because it is also told that when the dust had cleared—when all the tribes had chosen their ears of corn—there was but one short, half-rotten ear of corn that no one wanted. And that's the corn of the Hopi, the short, blue ear of corn. But, in essence, what the story is talking about is the true spirit of Hopi, and that spirit is, I guess, being humble, being industrious, and being respectful of other people.

So what can I say? You know, I think that's very basic. But, as we all know, that spirit has fallen to the wayside because of technology, science. The Hopi also say that in the future that short, little blue ear of corn will save the world. And you can interpret that for whatever it means. Thank you.

JIM JUDGE: Thank you, Leigh. I would like to comment that I was very encouraged by the opening ceremony this morning when Governor Romer [Roy Romer of Colorado] very specifically addressed the need to go toward sustainable agriculture in this world, rather than continuing the overproduction and overexploitation of natural resources that we seem to be currently engaged in. So I think there's some hope, at least in certain quarters.

Are there other questions that anybody would like to ask any of us up here?

On the Governmental Structure of the Anasazi

AUDIENCE: My name is Richard Agee and I would like to address my questions to Ed and Leigh. What does legend tell you as to governmental structure of the communities in those days?

JIM JUDGE: I think the question—and, Ed, you can handle this—is what, for instance, does Zuni legend tell you about the governmental structure of the ancient ones?

ED LADD: The system as it stands now is not a system that we chose by choice. Instead, the current Pueblo governmental system is based on the Spanish system of government. The system that used to be there in place was a theocratic system of religious leaders. And they had a religious leader, the bow priest, who guided the people through the various cyclical events that took place as part of the system. The bow priest and the war chief were the disciplinarians. But, you know, we had no jails. We really had nothing to fear, because we had no crime. Suicide wasn't heard of.

Crime? A crime was committed when a person was found to be a witch. That was the worst crime that one could commit. If you committed a crime against your fellow Zuni, that was punishable by the gods. It wasn't punishable by the society, but it was punishable by the gods.

So the bow priest and the chiefs were the ruling organization.

But the system we now live under is the basic system of the *cacique,* [a religious leader who is] considered to be the head man, and the governor and his council. That's a Spanish-imposed system. But the older system was based on theocracy. That was a good system.

And when it came time to plant corn, the sun priest designated the time and period, and it was established, it was recognized, and it was respected.

The system was such that it was followed, so there was no real need for jails, no real need for trials. But the trials there were public, and were witchcraft trials. But those were abandoned about 1920 or 1928. The last one was about in that period of time.

JIM JUDGE: Were there any lawyers, Ed?

ED LADD: No lawyers. We had Indian chiefs, we had Indian chiefs and doctors, but no lawyers.

JIM JUDGE: Are there any other questions to be addressed?

Volcanic Eruptions—A Cause of Abandonment?

AUDIENCE: My name is Sharon Mays. I'm one of the tour guides through Indian country on the Amtrak train, on the route between Gallup and Albuquerque that travels through El Malpais. And that's basically what my question is going to be centered on. Like Ed and Leigh, I really appreciate—as a modern Native American—the oral histories that we have in our tribe. And in reference to El Malpais, in talking to older Ácomas, they have told me these stories that they have in their tribe about a flowing river of fire, and also about a time of black air and of breathing what they describe as like ash. And the dating—the three times that I've been given the dating—of anywhere from 800 to 1,000 years [ago] when that major lava flow occurred. And the source of the lava, I'm told, was Mt. Taylor.

And my question is, because the whole area is just riddled with ruins, starting from the Gallup area all the way past Laguna—and you've been touching off and on about the possibility of changes in the environment—could that have possibly been a contributor of why those people left those ruins in that area? And were there other areas where there was volcanic activity going on?

ED LADD: Yes, there was. There was other volcanic activity, yes. And I think it's a pretty well known fact that Sunset Crater, which created a volcanic area in Arizona, erupted in—what year? 1100? I don't know what year. But we refer to that period of time as ________—that means "putrid" in Zuni. Putrid air came from the west and killed off many hundreds of people. And the people that ran and got away from it moved eastward. And they were going to return.

So there is tradition and there is a history of volcanic activity in that area that has to do with, I guess, the gases from the volcanic eruption that caused the deaths of many, many hundreds of people. According to the story, they even tried to alleviate the gas by covering a bowl of water and trying to breathe the water from the steam to try and get away from the gases from the eruption.

But the volcanic activity in El Malpais I think is a little bit out of the [time] range of the Indian people of that area. I think their ruins are probably—what? Pueblo III, Pueblo II? They're probably . . . the lava flow was probably several thousands of years earlier. So that area was not really very affected by the volcanic flow. But Sunset Crater was . . . it very definitely affected the area.

JIM JUDGE: I'm just wondering, does anybody know when the Mt. Taylor flow, the Malpais flow started? I think it's post-Pleistocene, but I don't really know. Does anybody know?

ED LADD: I think it's several thousand years ago.

JIM JUDGE: Several thousand. Does that answer your question? Thank you very much.

[Editor's note: The question asked from the audience evidently had to do with the prominent lava flows located south and east of Grants, New Mexico. Those flows are generally called "the *malpais*," and the greater part of them is within El Malpais National Monument. The lava flows—all quite similar basalts but extruded from different points of eruption—are of Pleistocene and Recent (post-Pleistocene) age. The flow that is probably youngest, the McCartys Flow, is inferred to be about 1,000 years old. The inference is based on Ácoma legends and on the occurrence of archaeological material in nearby valley fill that has been correlated to valley fill beneath the lava. Part of the McCartys Flow is visible from

Detail of "Mancos Black-on-White" dipper. Anasazi Heritage Center.

Amtrak trains.

Anasazi sites in the vicinity, some of them closely adjacent to the lava, are believed to have been established after the lava flows occurred. They are classified Pueblo II and Pueblo III. One prominent site, Las Ventanas ruin, is a Chacoan outlier dated approximately A.D. 1050–1200.

The questioner and the panelists both mistakenly spoke of the above-mentioned lava flows as "the Mt. Taylor flow." Mt. Taylor is a volcanic mountain north of Grants, but the successive eruptions and flows that created it occurred no later than Tertiary time. Basalt flows that are now exposed on high mesas around the flanks of Mt. Taylor, overlooking the McCartys Flow but much older, have yielded potassium-argon ages of 2.3 to 3.5 million years. See Charles H. Maxwell, *Geologic Map of El Malpais Lava Field and Surrounding Areas, Cibola County, New Mexico* (U.S. Geological Survey Misc. Investigations Series, Map I-1595), 1986.

Sunset Crater, in a rugged volcanic field northeast of Flagstaff, Arizona, is well known in both the geological and archaeological literature. It is a cinder cone that erupted violently in A.D. 1065, inundating the area with ash and driving away the prehistoric people of the vicinity. Evidently the ash was later found to enhance agriculture by serving as a mulch, so that considerable numbers of prehistoric people were attracted back to the area. See Harold S. Colton, *Black Sand: Prehistory in Northern Arizona* (Albuquerque: University of New Mexico Press), 1960; and Albert H. Schroeder, *Of Men and Volcanoes: The Sinagua of Northern Arizona* (Globe, Arizona: Southwest Parks and Monuments Association), 1977. However, newer studies and reevaluations suggest that the effects of the volcanic activity on prehistoric population and cultural change were neither so great nor so direct as was postulated earlier. See Peter J. Pilles, Jr., "Sunset Crater and the Sinagua: a New Interpretation," in *Volcanic Activity and Human Ecology*, edited by Payson D. Sheets and Donald Grayson (New York: Academic Press), 1979, pp. 459–85.

The Sunset Crater area has numerous archaeological sites, some of them large. Wupatki and other post-eruption ruins are the major features of nearby Wupatki National Monument.]

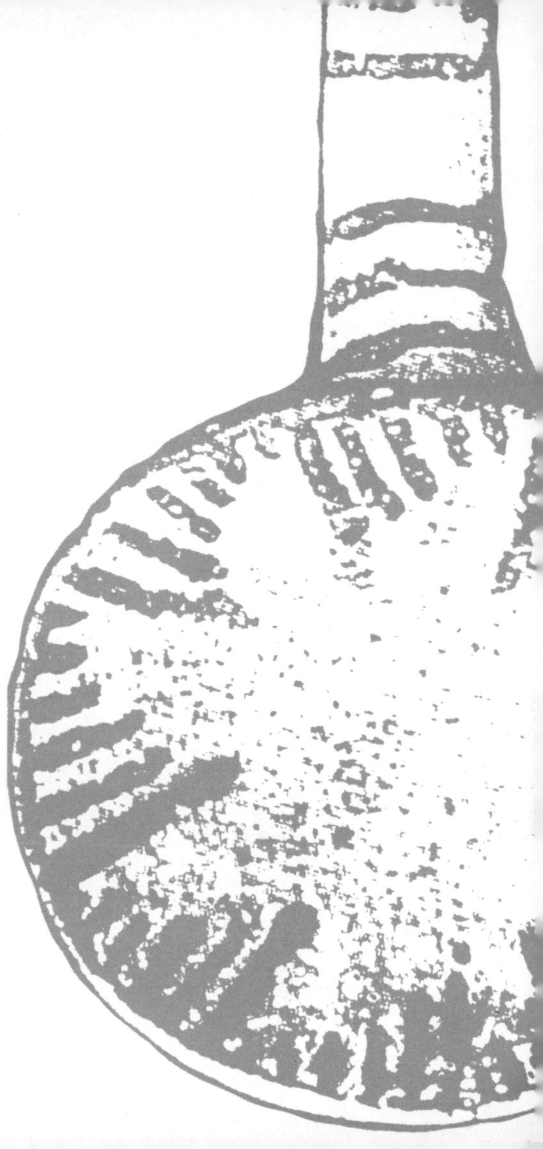

Did the Anasazi Seek a Spiritual Center?

AUDIENCE: First of all, I'd like to say that I really appreciated the comments of the representative of the Zuni Tribe. [*Turning to Mr. Ladd*] And I think your comments apply not only to Zuni, and not only to Anasazi—or whatever term you would like to apply to the ancient ones. But your idea of people looking for a spiritual center I think applies to each and every one of us. We may not be moving around, but I think we are all involved in this process of finding a spiritual center.

My question is actually for any of the other four archaeologists who commented, Anglo archaeologists. If you could give as honest a reply as possible, how much weight do you throw into this theory of large groups of people looking for a spiritual center? You have made lots of comments on the pottery style, on archaeological or agricultural patterns, things of that sort. But, as I say, I would like to get an honest response to this spiritual center theory—so to speak—and what kind of weight do you give to that?

JIM JUDGE: We're going to ask George Gumerman to respond to that.

GEORGE GUMERMAN: We have heard a lot of people, several of you in the audience, and the two anchors down on the end here [Jenkins and Ladd], about the value of oral tradition. And I personally feel that archaeologists have not given enough credence to oral tradition. I think some of this has to do with the uncritical acceptance of oral tradition in the late 1800s and early 1900s by archaeologists. My feeling, my honest feeling, is that oral tradition, simply stated such as "this is what we believe," is fine as long as it's considered a statement of belief and not fact.

For me it's something that's very important and that should probably be tested and evaluated. I am not asking the people who are talking about their oral tradition to evaluate their oral tradition. For them it's a matter of faith. It's a matter of personal knowledge. But I do, myself, feel that these . . . this kind of oral tradition, has to be evaluated in a rigorous fashion.

In terms of the written tradition of my own background, I have not personally evaluated it, but I do not believe that Jonah was swallowed by a whale. Nor do I believe that Noah took a male and a female of each animal onto the Ark. That's something that some people believe as an article of faith. I would like to see it tested. Some people have actually looked for the Ark.

BILL LIPE: Can I make a comment, Jim?

JIM JUDGE: Sure.

BILL LIPE: It seems to me that the general kind of scientific approach we're committed to is one that is only a partial way of knowing things. We try to deal with questions that can be framed in such ways that you can get some physical-data evidence on them. And there are only certain questions that we're smart enough to frame that way. So it's a fairly partial way of understanding things. However, it's been a way of understanding things that's been pretty productive in this society. It's probably pushing its limits in a field like anthropology, but we're still committed to trying to do it. But I don't think that anybody who is using a scientific approach should or could claim to be able to understand everything, or to be able to test all ideas. It may be that the traditional accounts are absolutely true, but it's often difficult to figure out a way to get data that would allow you to test them.

JIM JUDGE: I would like to follow that, too. The archaeologists look for what we call the archaeological or material correlates of behavior. And, as the gentleman who asked the question pointed out, each of us is looking for—or wandering perhaps—but looking for a central place. And, if you examine your own behavior, what kind of material correlates are you leaving for some archaeologist 2,000 years hence? It's very, very difficult to verify those kinds of things archaeologically. Perhaps we're all simplistic, but we look for things we can verify more easily and try to be more sure about. The subjective interpretation of the archaeological record is one which anybody can do, actually. And, as you may know, it's hard to get archaeologists to agree on anything, but the more objective we become, the more likely it is that we can agree on certain conclusions.

Are there other questions?

LINDA CORDELL: May I say something?

JIM JUDGE: Oh, certainly, Linda.

LINDA CORDELL: I do just want to respond to that, also, a little bit. I agree, obviously, with my colleagues that, as scientists, we buy into a system that allows us one way of tending to confirm relationships, or "disconfirm" them. And that is the method we use. On the other hand, archaeologists who work in the Americas are generally anthropologists, so that one of the ways that we look at understanding the world, and test ideas, is through comparative studies of people throughout the world. My comment just relates to the fact that we do have to evaluate things on the basis of empirical evidence, because that's how we are defined and constrained in our scholarship. On the other hand, every story of migration that one hears—and that has been collected and recorded among the Pueblos—describes exactly the kind of phenomenon that we would expect . . . of groups separating, of people coming together, of people being all over a landscape.

And, in a general sense, yes, that's what it looks like. It's unfortunate that we don't know what language was spoken where, or what all the material correlates of it were, and who went to exactly which place. It gets very complex, in that there will not be a good dialogue on understanding, because there are different ways of understanding. But there is a dialogue about the kinds of stories that are told in oral traditions that would help us understand more about the record.

DAVE BRETERNITZ: Let me just say that what we see in the archaeological record, and what we have come to appreciate as archaeologists, and as knowledgeable laymen, and as "current residents," is the fact that the northern Four Corners area is a marginal one in which to make a living, both now and in the past. The Anasazi were tremendously adaptable; they made a living in this marginally agricultural area for a long period of time, but utilizing very local situations. The people who lived on the Mesa Verde had a different set of soils, a different rainfall pattern, a different drainage pattern, and different agricultural potential than did the Anasazi who lived in the Montezuma valley around Cortez, or the earlier Anasazi who resided in the Dolores River valley. The diverse geology, physiography, and environment fostered a great many local adaptations by the Anasazi.

To say that one set of Anasazi responded to a set of circumstances like all the others—that there is a general pattern—is something that just doesn't show up in the local archaeological record. And I will point out this fact by showing that people who may even have spoken the same language, and who had potential of day-to-day contact with each other, responded to a common set of circumstances in different manners.

From the Dolores Archaeological Project we have two Pueblo I villages that were built and occupied contemporaneously in the late A.D. 800s and early 900s. The evidence indicates that there was a time of stress in the early 900s, probably because there was less rainfall, a shorter growing season, and therefore less land available that would potentially make a crop. There was a stress upon the available agricultural land. But, in these two villages, within about five miles of one another, the inhabitants responded to their stresses in differing ways. In one village, in order to maintain their established way of life, a group of people moved out; they emigrated. Some of the population left so that those who remained could continue to exist as they were accustomed to doing on the decreased amount of available agricultural land.

In the other village the people left altogether, on a permanent basis. They only returned to occupy the site seasonally, during the summer. They lived else-

Detail of "Mesa Verde Black-on-White" mug. Mesa Verde National Park.

where during the winter.

This example is substantiated by archaeological evidence. I'm certain in my own mind that these people from the two villages spoke to one another, that they may have exchanged marriage partners, that they shared a similar religious, social, economic, and political system. Yet they responded to a similar set of circumstances in different ways. When we speak in generalities we tend to forget that not everybody, or every group of people, responds in the same way to the same, or similar, circumstances.

But it still goes without saying that at about A.D. 1300, in the northern San Juan, for whatever reason, the Anasazi left. And they didn't come back. They still exist, as the Hopi and the Zuni and the Rio Grande Pueblos, but these people do not live up here; they are gone.

I suggest that we do not make a one-to-one correlation between the Anasazi and the Hopi/Zuni/Rio Grande Pueblos any more than we make a one-to-one correlation of Anglo-Saxon, Norman, and Celtic with modern Britons.

JIM JUDGE: Thank you. I realize that this was scheduled from 6:30 to 8:30. I'd like to take a few more questions, if there's an interest in asking them. And I know we'll stay up here for them.

Anasazi Migration—What of Navajo Legend and Religion?

AUDIENCE: Thank you. I'm a member of the Navajo Tribe. And it's very interesting to listen to you gentlemen while at the same time I'm trying to compare some of the comments to my upbringing about the Navajo genesis. And, in a lot of respects all three [?], since we live in the same area, the history is pretty familiar, similar. And there was a lot behind what was mentioned earlier about each of the tribes trying to find their center or their place of . . . where they're supposed to be, and they only had a certain amount of time to do that.

We have a similar story with the Navajos, also. Some of them were never able to find where they were supposed to be, and they ended up in Canada. And we have Navajos that call themselves the [inaudible], that talk pretty much like we

Detail of "Sosi Black-on-White" jar. From Black Mesa, Arizona.

do. And we have stories that cover that.

But my question to . . . I would like to pose it to Leigh, or to the gentleman from the Zuni . . . is this: I've heard stories about the different villages, about the First Mesa and Second Mesa villages representing the different portions of the body of an Indian who was lying from east to west. You know, I remember that story very vaguely even from the time I was a small child. And I wonder if there was any . . . is there any significance to that story from your own teachings and learnings from your fathers?

And that's basically my question. Because I think maybe somewhere along the line a lot of the stories [of various tribes] are the same. And I'd just like to question that.

The other thing . . . the Navajos, like our religious people have been teaching us about the Anasazi . . . is that they're not . . . you know, we don't call them Anasazi [*'anaasází*]. We call them *Ana'sa za'*. And that's a more recent term. But I've been asking my grandfather what that means, "Anasazi." Their most common term, they call it "the ancient ones." But I think that some of the terms that were used 'way back some time ago are beginning to be lost, because I ask a lot of these older Navajos, and they don't seem to know what that word actually meant, "Anasazi." And, this . . . we're losing a lot of the . . . our cultural aspects of the meaning and the significance behind some of the words of the songs, the prayers, and our history, our genesis.

But most of our religious leaders have always told us that the reason why the Anasazi don't live in these areas anymore is because they basically forgot about their religious life and their religious activities. And they sort of got in disfavor with the mandate that was given them when they were placed on this earth. And, as a result, nature was released on them. That's the reason they were scattered.

And I don't know if that's just what our religious people tell us. Maybe, in a way, they're trying to tell us that we need to maintain our religious values, in order to survive as a race. Because, if we don't have a religious value to hand down to our kids and teach our kids, we won't be very much of a human being. We'll sort of be just like animals. And maybe that's what they were trying to teach us in telling us that this is what happened.

But I'd just like to mention that. I don't know what your teaching or your [tradition] might be from your perspective, from your tribes. But I would sure like to share that with both the Zuni and the Hopi panelists. Thank you.

JIM JUDGE: Thank you for the Navajo view. Leigh, do you want to say anything about that?

LEIGH JENKINS: I guess in response to the specific question whether or not there's any symbolism of the Hopi villages, or the mesas, representing a view of either a male . . . or the human race being represented in that fashion . . . I don't know of any, really, specifically . . . on anything relative to any of the legends that are told.

All I can really respond with is the fact that the clans represent much of the directional travels of the Hopi. I really don't have any specific comment back to that question.

JIM JUDGE: Are there any other comments or questions to be made?

Kokopelli—A Link from Past to Present?

AUDIENCE: My name is Robert Beers. I would like to hear some comments on the image of Kokopelli, the ancient kokopelli, and how far-reaching—or what linkage there may be with the modern tribes?

JIM JUDGE: Ed Ladd would like to take that.

Kokopelli petroglyph. La Cieneguilla area, New Mexico.

ED LADD: Kokopelli, huh? Kokopelli is probably one of the oldest deities in the pantheon of gods and spirits in the whole of the Southwest. It appears very early in the rock art symbols in both the southern area and up north of here. And almost every place you go you may find the kokopelli present, with his very manly attributes so exposed. He's a fertility symbol.

As far as I know, there is no representation of the kokopelli in a modern period . . . except for one ceremony that has not been performed in the Zuni culture for maybe—oh, seventy-five or a hundred years. I've only been told that this is one of the ceremonies that used to be held representing the kokopelli symbol and the fertility rites of the group. But as far as the symbol itself is concerned, it's one of the oldest ones that I've found in the area. And I'm not sure if there is any real cultural connection that occurs among the Hopis. It [the kokopelli] occurs among the Zunis. It occurs in the Rio Grande areas. So it is most universal.

LEIGH JENKINS: To this day the Hopi people do, in fact, represent that particular pictograph, or petroglyph, that we find symbolized through the . . . I guess the Hopi pronunciation is "socapella." That's basically how the Hopi say it, "socapella." And we do have a kachina [Kokopelli] to this day that dances. And I do agree with Mr. Ladd here that it does represent fertility. But more specifically, it represents the rejuvenation of life.

[Editor's note: The kokopelli is a mythical humpbacked creature often portrayed playing a flute and dancing to its tune. The figure appears in prehistoric Anasazi rock art and as a motif on painted pottery. The kokopelli is frequently depicted with a phallus and is known as a symbol of fecundity.

Several short publications discuss the kokopelli, including Mischa Titiev, "The Story of Kokopele," *American Anthropologist*, vol. 41 (1939), pp. 91–98; and Etienne B. Renaud, "Kokopelli, a Study in Pueblo Mythology," *Southwestern Lore*, vol. 14 (1948), pp. 25–40. The Titiev article mentions Hopi ceremonial dances performed in the 1930s that included impersonations of the kokopelli.

Additional details and discussions of the kokopelli appear in Campbell Grant, *The Rock Art of the North American Indian* (New York: Thomas Y. Crowell), 1967; and in K. F. Wellmann, "Kokopelli of Indian Paleology: Hunchbacked Rain Priest,

Hunting Magician, and Don Juan of the Old Southwest," *Journal of the American Medical Association*, vol. 212 (1970), pp. 1,678–82.]

JIM JUDGE: Thank you very much. It's getting late and dark. One more question and then let's call it a day. Does anybody have another question?

Anasazi Intentions—To Leave Forever?

AUDIENCE: I think there needs to be at least two more questions asked tonight. I'm Pete Christensen from Grand Junction.

I am not an archaeologist, or a Hopi, or Zuni. I'm relying on what I see in the Anasazi Heritage Center, such as the everyday-living objects. And, going on what Dr. Cordell said, that you cannot rely upon what you see in excavations as to explanations on why the Anasazi left the area . . . why is it, according to Mr. Ladd—if the Indians were seeking religious satisfaction and moving in periods of every four years—why do we see everyday-living objects and artifacts left behind?

JIM JUDGE: George Gumerman knows why so many pieces of pottery were left behind.

GEORGE GUMERMAN: No, I don't. But what I find fascinating is the very question of what we characterize as "abandonment." In some cases, in the last occupation near Navajo Mountain, for example, we have found the *metates*, the grinding stones for corn, lined up against the wall, and every one of them purposely broken. That find suggests that they knew they were leaving, that they weren't coming back, and that they broke their tools so nobody else could use them. In other cases, such as on northern Black Mesa, after twenty years of excavation—after excavating hundreds of rooms from the last occupation, and finding many worn-out *metates*—no whole or purposely broken *metates* were found. They took them wherever they were going. Of course, these are very heavy artifacts, and the raw material is available everywhere. So those people apparently knew where they were going, and it wasn't very far.

In other cases, in the White Mountains country of central Arizona, in some of the rooms you can see where a man was sitting down in a corner sharpening a projectile point, or a knife. There was a crescent of tiny little chips of stone there. Corn was left in the vessels and pots were on the floor. It looks like everybody went out to work that day and never came back.

In other words, we see these very great variations of how people abandoned a region. It's a fascinating story, because each one tells a little different story.

BILL LIPE: Can I make a comment, Jim? In *this* area, and particularly on the Dolores Project sites, which date primarily to the A.D. 800s—and also in some of the Crow Canyon work that we're doing in sites that date to the 1200s—we find a common pattern of abandonment. That pattern involved the people cleaning up the sites pretty well, sometimes even taking the roof beams. It looks like there were still people living in the area, and that those who moved were probably not moving very far. But then we find in both those time periods, at the end of occupation, a tendency to leave lots of things in the sites, including unbroken and quite usable material. And often some of the structures were burned. So it might have to do with . . . well, the amount of pottery left may have to do with how far the people were going and whether there were still some people in the area or not.

JIM JUDGE: Ed Ladd?

ED LADD: The one thing is . . . I'm not talking about the roof beams, or anything like that. I'm talking about the *metates* and other objects. You'll find a lot of broken objects in archaeological sites. And even now, today, we consider the fact that, if an object is broken . . . ah, you've heard the words "you can't take it with you"? You can't take it with you. Well, this is the way to take it with you. It's spiritually broken. It is . . . once an object is broken, it belongs to "the other side." And so much of it had to do with religion and religious attitudes in the breaking of tools and the breaking of objects for purposes of spiritually giving it up. So, obviously, it's exactly the same thing. It's to allow the spirit to escape and allow the spirit not to come back. And I'm sure that much of the broken pottery, and the ritual breaking of the potteries in the Chaco Canyon, was basically that same idea. And it was probably sent to the [other] world by breaking it. And if you pick up a cup, and it all of a sudden breaks in your hand, that means that somebody on the other side wanted it. And so it's sent. So a lot of the broken objects were spiritually dispatched, once they were broken.

JIM JUDGE: "God made me do it," right? Did you have another question, sir?

AUDIENCE: No, I didn't. Thank you for your comments.

JIM JUDGE: Shela?

On the Future of Four Corners Archaeology

AUDIENCE: I'm Shela McFarlin with the Anasazi Heritage Center. I have a few remaining questions, as I think you might have. I would like to know, What do you do next? What's the future of Four Corners archaeology? What evidence do you look for? Where do we go from here? Or are we finished with this issue?

JIM JUDGE: Those aren't easy questions, Shela. Hmm, I'd like each archaeologist to respond very briefly to that.

I myself am going to say that I have the good fortune of . . . I'm going to move to Durango and teach at Fort Lewis College and be able to use the field school to dig in the Pigge Chaco site next to the Lowry ruin. And I hope to continue research in this vein, and be instructed and guided by my colleagues in terms of asking relevant questions of the archaeological record. And above and beyond that—I think this may be a little bit different from my past view of future archaeology—I think it's very, very important, if not essential, that we archaeologists involve the public and the public's views more and more in our work and research, to interest the public in what we do, to inform the public as to what

Detail of "Mancos Black-on-White" dipper. Anasazi Heritage Center.

we do, to engage the public in our activities. And I know I feel committed to doing that, at least in the activities that I hope to pursue in the near future.

Let's get back in order. Dave, what are you going to do, now that you're retired?

DAVE BRETERNITZ: I think one of the fruitful areas of archaeological inquiry is the examination of abandonment processes. Why do we find that some houses were burned? Why do we find that some houses are full of stuff and some are almost devoid of artifacts? What behavorial aspects are involved? Abandonment processes appear to be different if people plan to leave temporarily, as opposed to permanently, and if they move a short or a relatively long distance. Study of abandonment may help us answer the basic questions asked of this panel—"Where did the people go and why did they go and when did they go?" What they left behind and what they took with them should help answer these prevailing questions. But we have to dig a lot of sites and do detailed documentation. These investigations will take a long time and we have just begun to collect the kinds of data that will help us.

I believe the investigation of abandonment processes is going to be a very interesting and fruitful aspect of future archaeology in the Four Corners area.

Finally, we are going to have to acknowledge the increasing body of information that indicates strife, i.e., warfare, in the northern Southwest in the late 1200s.

JIM JUDGE: Linda?

LINDA CORDELL: In a general sense, is there anything left to do in the Four Corners? I think all of us would say, "Of course there is." You know, archaeology is certainly not going to die, we hope. And we hope that you, the public, will be interested enough to keep it going by paying taxes and other things.

I would point out, and I think Dave is correct, that since the beginning of the '70s there has been more archaeology done in this area—done with a variety of new techniques and tools—and people are asking more difficult questions of

the data. And I think that will certainly continue.

I expect to continue working on "where they went" rather than on "where they came from." I'm looking at how much they resembled what was here, organizationally, and how much was different and changed [in] that environment.

JIM JUDGE: George?

GEORGE GUMERMAN: I would like to take a little broader perspective than just the Four Corners area in answering interesting questions—about how cultures change and evolve and how simple agricultural societies change through time. The amount of information that we have here [in the Four Corners] is wonderful, and our data base is so great, that I think we can use this information for talking about human beings in general in this kind of environment, with this kind of technology, to understand human behavior in very general terms. . . . And that's a very general answer.

JIM JUDGE: Bill?

BILL LIPE: Well, I think the question we've posed tonight has to do with the abandonment of the northern Anasazi area, the northern Four Corners area in the 1200s, with movement to an area farther south. So it's a big-scale question. As some of us pointed out, most of our work has tended to be on a smaller scale. I think we've gotten pretty good at talking about how people lived—especially about how people made a living in particular locations. I think a lot of people have addressed that. But this is a bigger-scale question. So we need to survey the literature Southwestwide, and we need to cooperate more among the archaeologists working in this area, and among the archaeologists working in New Mexico and Arizona. That's one answer.

Second, I think we need to frame the question better, so we have several alternatives that we can rank in terms of evidence. I think we need to frame the

Detail of "Mesa Verde Black-on-White" bowl. From Mug House, Mesa Verde National Park.

alternatives of "were they pushed out?" or "were they attracted to" better or different conditions farther south? We need to frame that in terms of how we can get evidence that would allow us at least to say whether one alternative is more plausible than another.

So I think it's a scale question. It's a question of larger scale than we are used to, and we need to develop ideas and collaborate with one another to address questions at that scale and get out of our local area, and go beyond the kind of approach that we've invested in during the last few years.

JIM JUDGE: I would ask the two tribal representatives to comment very briefly on where they would like to see archaeologists—no, not *archaeologists* go, but where *archaeology* should go. That was a loaded question.

ED LADD: Well, we'll keep trying to tell you what happened, but I guess you won't believe us anyway.

LEIGH JENKINS: I suppose tribes and archaeology can become really viable partners. And I hope that the efforts of archaeology truly represent the interests of the cultures that these lands represent.

And I'll end with a short note saying that I think that, as protectors of these cultural resources—you know, a culture may be intrinsic to a society, like the Hopi people, for example. But still, now the cultural resources are *everybody's* heritage. For the record, we should be proud that we hold some of the richest archaeological information, right here in the Southwest. And we're all in this together. The heritage that archaeology reveals is your heritage as well as mine. Thank you.

JIM JUDGE: I'd simply like to close by thanking the BLM, and especially Shela McFarlin for the incredible job she did in organizing this panel and getting us all together. And I'd like to thank the panel, and particularly the audience, for your endurance and your participation. Thank you very much.

The Panelists

Dr. W. JAMES JUDGE began his teaching career at Colorado State University. Later, however, he became a faculty member at the University of New Mexico, where he had earned his Ph.D. in anthropology. While there he directed the Chaco Project for the National Park Service from 1977 to 1985. Dr. Judge has more recently served as director of the Southern Methodist University research and educational facility near Taos, New Mexico. In 1990 he joined the faculty of the Department of Anthropology at Fort Lewis College, Durango, Colorado.

Dr. DAVID A. BRETERNITZ received his Ph.D. in anthropology at the University of Arizona. Now retired from the faculty of the University of Colorado, he lives in Dove Creek, Colorado, where he pursues several interests in archaeology. Dr. Breternitz's distinguished career includes service as principal investigator for the Dolores Archaeological Program from 1978 to 1985. That program was one of the largest federally sponsored archaeological investigations ever undertaken.

Dr. LINDA S. CORDELL is curator of anthropology at the California Academy of Sciences in San Francisco. She received her Ph.D. from the University of California, Santa Barbara, with a dissertation based largely on Mesa Verde, Colorado. Thereafter, Dr. Cordell undertook extensive field work in New Mexico, where she was on the faculty of the University of New Mexico. She is the author of the popular and now-standard textbook on Southwest archaeology, *Prehistory of the Southwest*.

Dr. GEORGE J. GUMERMAN earned his Ph.D. in anthropology at the University of Arizona. For many years he served as director of the Black Mesa Project in northeastern Arizona, which was a large, intensive archaeological project described in several works, including Dr. Gumerman's own book, *A View from Black Mesa*. Dr. Gumerman is also professor of anthropology and director of the Center for Archaeological Investigations at Southern Illinois University.

LEIGH JENKINS serves the Hopi Tribe as tribal cultural preservation officer. In that capacity he shares dual insights as a Hopi tribal member and as the manager of nationally significant cultural resources. Mr. Jenkins is a graduate of Northern Arizona University in business administration, and he has been assistant director of the Hopi Tribal Health Department.

EDMUND J. LADD is curator of ethnology at the Museum of New Mexico's Laboratory of Anthropology in Santa Fe. He earlier retired from the National Park Service, where he was a staff archaeologist in Hawaii. Mr. Ladd brings a unique perspective as both a member of the Zuni Tribe and as a scientist. He holds a master's degree in anthropology from the University of New Mexico.

Dr. WILLIAM LIPE is currently professor of anthropology at Washington State University and director of research at the Crow Canyon Archaeological Center near Cortez, Colorado. He received his Ph.D. in anthropology from Yale University. Dr. Lipe's research has included the Dolores Archaeological Program as well as projects in the Glen Canyon and Cedar Mesa areas of Utah.

Further Reading

Ambler, J. Richard. *The Anasazi: Prehistoric People of the Four Corners Region*. Flagstaff: Museum of Northern Arizona, third ed. 1977.

Breternitz, David A., C. K. Robinson and G. T. Gross (compilers). *Dolores Archaeological Program: Final Synthetic Report*. Denver: USDI Bureau of Reclamation, 1986.

Brody, Jerry J. *Anasazi*. New York: Rizzoli, 1990.

Canby, Thomas Y. "The Anasazi, Riddles in the Ruins," *National Geographic*, Vol. 162, No. 5 (May 1982), pp. 554–92.

Cordell, Linda S. *Prehistory of the Southwest*. Orlando, Florida: Academic Press, 1984.

Dozier, Edward P. *The Pueblo Indians of North America*. New York: Holt, Rinehart and Winston, 1970.

Ferguson, William M., and Arthur H. Rohn. *Anasazi Ruins of the Southwest in Color.* Albuquerque: University of New Mexico Press, 1987.

Gaede, Marc (photographer), and Marnie Gaede (ed.). *Camera, Spade and Pen: An Inside View of Southwestern Archaeology.* Tucson: University of Arizona Press, 1978.

Gumerman, George J. *A View from Black Mesa*. Tucson: University of Arizona Press, 1984.

———. *Anasazi in a Changing Environment*. School of American Research Advanced Seminar Series. Cambridge: Cambridge University Press, 1988.

Judge, W. James. "New Light on Chaco Canyon," in *New Light on Chaco Canyon*, edited by David Grant Noble. Santa Fe: School of American Research, 1984.

Kidder, Alfred V. *An Introduction to the Study of Southwestern Archaeology.* New Haven:

Yale University Press, rev. ed. 1962.
Ladd, Edmund J. "Zuni Religion and Philosophy," in *Zuni/El Morro: Past and Present*, edited by David Grant Noble. Santa Fe: School of American Research, 1983.
Lipe, William D. "The Southwest," in *Ancient Native North Americans*, edited by Jesse D. Jennings. San Francisco: W. H. Freeman, 1978.
——— (ed.). *The Architecture of Social Integration in Prehistoric Pueblos*. Cortez, Colorado: Crow Canyon Archaeological Center, 1989.
Lister, Robert H., and Florence C. Lister. *Those Who Came Before*. Tucson: Southwest Parks and Monuments Association, 1983.
Martin, Paul S., and Fred T. Plog. *The Archaeology of Arizona*. Garden City, N.Y.: Doubleday, 1973.
Matlock, Gary. *Enemy Ancestors: The Anasazi World*. Flagstaff, Arizona: Northland Press, 1988.
Noble, David Grant. *Ancient Ruins of the Southwest*. Flagstaff, Arizona: Northland Press, 1981.
——— (ed.). *Bandelier National Monument*. Santa Fe: School of American Research, 1980.
——— (ed.). *Understanding the Anasazi of Mesa Verde and Hovenweep*. Santa Fe: School of American Research, 1985.
——— (ed.). *Pecos Ruins*. Santa Fe: School of American Research, 1981.
——— (ed.). *Tsé Yaa Kin: Houses Beneath the Rock* [Canyon de Chelly and Navajo national monuments]. Santa Fe: School of American Research, 1986.
Ortiz, Alfonso (ed.). *Handbook of North American Indians, Southwest*. Vol. 9 of a series. Washington, D.C.: Smithsonian Institution, 1979.
Powell, Shirley, and George J. Gumerman. *People of the Mesa: The Archaeology of Black Mesa, Arizona*. Tucson and Carbondale: Southwest Parks and Monuments Association and Southern Illinois University Press, 1987.
Schaafsma, Polly. *Indian Rock Art of the Southwest*. Albuquerque: University of New Mexico Press, 1980.
Waters, Frank. *Book of the Hopi*. New York: Penguin Books, 1963, reprint 1982.

Chronology, Greater Four Corners Area

William D. Lipe
Director of Research
Crow Canyon
Archaeological Center
Cortez, Colorado

10,000(?)–6500 B.C.

Paleo-Indian

Small bands of hunters and gatherers, preying upon late-Pleistocene megafauna (e.g., mammoth, large bison) when available. Cooler, drier environments, becoming like those of the present by end of period. Human population density very low, settlement mobility very high. Distinctive large, well-made, lanceolate spear points; ground stone rare or not present. Paleo-Indian evidence in Four Corners almost exclusively from small surface campsites and isolated projectile point finds.

6500–1500 B.C.

Archaic

Subsistence based on wild foods hunted and gathered in environments generally like those of present. Natural shelters and open campsites used in seasonal round. Storage pits present, but not common. Lightly built house structures probably used at some sites, but rarely preserved archaeologically. Low population density. Atlatl and dart the principal weapons. No pottery.

1500 B.C.–A.D. 50

Basketmaker I (early)

Long-term seasonal (?) use of caves for camping, storage, burial, rock art. Camp and limited-activity sites in open. San Juan Anthropomorphic–style pictographs and petroglyphs. No pottery. Atlatl and dart; large, corner- or side-notched projectile points. Elaborate, coiled and twined basketry. Corn and squash grown, but no beans; cultivation primarily floodplain or runoff based (?). Hunting/gathering probably important; population density low relative to later periods, but higher than Archaic.

A.D. 50–500

Basketmaker II (late)

Habitations are shallow pithouses plus separate storage pits or cists; dispersed settlement with small, low-density villages in some areas; caves and campsites important as well (?). No pottery. Atlatl and dart are principal weapons. Reliance on maize and squash agriculture, but beans not grown. Upland dry farming in addition to floodplain farming.

A.D. 500–750

Basketmaker III

Habitations are deep pithouses, often with antechamber, and with separate storage pits, cists, or small *jacal* surface structures. Dispersed settlement with occasional small villages and occasional great kivas. Plain gray pottery, small frequencies of black and white. Bow and arrow replace atlatl. Beans added to cultigens.

A.D. 750–900

Pueblo I

Large villages in some areas; dispersed settlement in others. Habitation units of "protokiva" pit structure with vent shaft, plus surface room block of storage and living rooms; *jacal* or crude masonry construction. Great kivas present in many communities. Plain and neck-banded gray pottery abundant, with low frequencies of black-and-white and decorated red ware. Notched pebble axes common.

A.D. 900–1150

Pueblo II

Chacoan florescence: "great houses," elaborate great kivas, roads, etc. in many but not all regions; strong differences between great houses and surrounding "unit pueblos" composed of masonry-lined kivas and surface masonry room blocks. Corrugated gray and elaborate black-and-white pottery widespread, plus decorated red or orange types in some areas. Period of maximum northern and western extent of Pueblo culture in Four Corners area.

A.D. 1150–1350

Pueblo III

Large pueblos and/or "revisionist great houses" in some areas, dispersed pattern in others; high kiva-to-room ratios. Cliff dwellings, towers, triwalls common in some areas. Corrugated gray and elaborate black-and-white pottery widespread, plus decorated red or orange pottery in some areas. Grooved axes common. Abandonment of the Four Corners by 1300; population increase to the south in Rio Grande, Hopi, Zuni, Mogollon Rim areas.

A.D. 1350–1600

Pueblo IV

Large, plaza-oriented pueblos in Rio Grande and western Pueblo areas; low kiva-to-room ratios. Kachina cult widespread. Corrugated pottery replaced by plain utility types; black and white declines relative to red, orange, or yellow types. Area occupied by Puebloans continues to shrink as Mogollon Rim abandoned. Many present-day Pueblo groups identifiable in this period; Athapaskans enter Four Corners area at this time.

A.D. 1600–present

Pueblo V

Puebloans adapt to Spanish presence in 17th and 18th centuries, to Anglo-Americans in 19th and 20th centuries. Population declines initially owing to European diseases, Spanish oppression, raiding by horse-mounted nomadic Indians. Pueblos incorporate many elements of European material and economic culture but tenaciously preserve languages, religion, aspects of social organization, and subsistence. Navajos expand into much of southern Four Corners. Indian craft arts revive and expand in response to tourism and market demand in 20th century.